The Importance of Being Fuzzy

*

The Importance of Being Fuzzy
and Other Insights from the Border between Math and Computers

*

ARTURO SANGALLI

PRINCETON UNIVERSITY PRESS

PRINCETON, NEW JERSEY

Library of Congress Cataloging-in-Publication Data

Sangalli, Arturo, 1940–
    The importance of being fuzzy : and other insights from the border
between math and computers / Arturo Sangalli.
        p. cm.
    Includes bibliographical references and index.
    ISBN 0-691-00144-8 (cl : alk. paper)
    1. Soft computing.   2. Fuzzy systems.   I. Title.
QA76.9.S63S26   1998   98-3818
006.3--dc21   CIP

This book has been composed in Palatino

The paper used in this publication meets the minimum requirements of
ANSI/NISO Z39.48-1992 (R1997) (*Permanence of Paper*)

http://pup.princeton.edu

Printed in the United States of America

1 3 5 7 9 10 8 6 4 2
(Pbk.)

* Contents *

CONTENTS

CONTENTS

* *Preface* *

PROBLEMS

"It looks as though the Germans are winning the war,"
I remarked.
"They will win, unless we can stop these losses—and stop
them soon," replied Admiral Jellicoe, commander of the British
Navy. (He was referring to the British and neutral shipping
losses of the last months: 536,000 tons in February 1917,
603,000 tons in March, and a predicted 900,000 tons in April.)
"Is there no solution for the problem?" I asked.
"Absolutely none that we can see now."
(A. J. Marder, in his historical account "From the
Dreadnought to Scapa Flow")[1]

From our point of view, we are aware of it and we're looking
at it and we're assessing whether or not we have a problem
and, if we do, what we should do about it.
(An Ontario Hydro spokesman, confirming, in January 1997,
that a corrosion problem might be afflicting the utility's
nuclear reactors)[2]

Houston, we have a problem . . .
(Commander Jim Lovell [Tom Hanks], in the MCA-Universal
film Apollo 13)

HUMANS and other living beings have been confronted with problems ever since the dawn of life, beginning with the most pressing of
all: staying alive. In the course of time, problems have grown in
variety and sophistication and have spread over the entire range of

human activities, from simple, everyday problems, to complex, far-reaching ones, threatening the welfare and even the survival of millions of people. But if problems are everywhere, so are solutions, which too often are taken for granted. Living organisms themselves, in their rich diversity, are multiple solutions to the difficult problem of surviving in a changing and often hostile environment.

The quality of life in developed societies is directly related to the ingenuity and resourcefulness of their problem-solving elites: scientists, engineers, managers, and other experts. Finding those often elusive solutions involves in many cases the use of mathematics and computers, sometimes to a significant degree. This is not only true in the physical sciences and engineering, but also in domains as diverse as administration, medicine, economics, or the social sciences. Consider, for instance, the current concern with the consequences of global warming, a problem that is not likely to be solved or go away in the near future. Climate experts have detected a rise of about 0.5 degree centigrade in the average surface temperature of our planet during the past hundred years. And scientists studying this phenomenon forecast a further rise of up to 3.5 degrees by the year 2100 if nothing is done to reduce emissions of the so-called greenhouse gases, which trap heat in the atmosphere. These forecasts were obtained by running computer simulations based on mathematical models of our ecosystem. Mathematics and computers in this particular case were not used to solve a problem but merely to warn us that we have one.

We live in the information age, which is rapidly becoming the era of information overload. The multiple problems arising from the need to handle vast quantities of data would be untractable without the help of mathematics and computing. Information can only be stored, processed, and retrieved if it is coded in one form or another. Before the computer can display a page of text such as this one, for instance, the letters of the alphabet, the punctuation marks, and so on must be coded as strings of binary digits. In the field of high-resolution TV, the enormous amount of information involved requires the encoding to be as economical as possible. The relevant techniques, known as data compression, are initially mathematical concepts before becoming electromagnetic signals and finally a picture on your television screen. The study and the design of codes is a branch of mathematics known as coding theory. Its general aim is to provide solutions to a problem posed by Claude Shannon, the father of the theory of information. "The fundamental problem of communication," wrote Shannon in 1948, "is that of reproducing at one point, either exactly or approximately, a message selected at another point."

Computers and mathematics also help to ensure the confidentiality of the information transmitted over telephone lines, computer networks, or other communication channels. One way to protect a message from undesired eyes or ears is to encode it so that, hopefully, only those for whom it is intended can understand it. The problem of devising secure encoding/decoding procedures (and of breaking them) belongs to the field of cryptography, which makes heavy use of mathematical ideas and techniques. As is the case with most problems, this one has many possible solutions, some better than others—more difficult to crack or easier to implement, for example. The encoding and decoding operations will likely require massive computation, making the use of computers essential if these operations are to be performed efficiently and fast. Once the message has been coded, its security may hinge on the practical impossibility of solving a mathematical riddle: that of finding the prime factors of very large numbers (over 200 numerals long, when written in decimal notation).

RECIPES THAT WORK

Mathematics, commonly (but incompletely) described as the science of size and number, provides us with tools for solving general problems, along with a language for formulating them precisely. Mathematicians thrive on problems and keep inventing new ones all the time, often for the simple pleasure of being able to solve them. Finding a complete solution may take years, and require the joint efforts of many of them. The search stops if someone discovers that no solution exists. But if the problem is finally solved, it immediately becomes history as far as the mathematician is concerned. For practically minded people, however, it is the solution that counts and how it can be exploited to help solve other, more mundane problems. These pragmatists usually care little about the elegance of the mathematical argument as long as the expected payoff is commensurate with the resources required (in time, money, etc.) to implement the solution.

Occasionally, solutions may create bigger problems than the ones they were supposed to solve. A recent book by historian Edward Tenner (*Why Things Bite Back: Technology and the Revenge of Unintended Consequences*) is a catalogue of solutions that backfired and technological plans gone thoroughly awry. Among these, the pesticides that were dispersed in the Southern United States during the 1950s and 1960s to eradicate the South American fire ant and ended up wiping out their predators, actually increasing the feared ant population.

Over the last few decades, our problem-solving ability has been considerably enhanced by the prodigious increase in the computing power available. This is not to say that theory has lagged behind or that it only plays a secondary part in the quest for solutions. Scratch the surface of a practical problem and you will often find another one that is mathematical in nature. In order to solve the former, you may well have to solve the latter first, usually by brain power alone. Nonetheless, as machines become smarter, their role in the solution process is gradually changing from that of mere assistants to one of active partners of the human expert. And it is not too far-fetched to imagine a reversal of roles in the future, with humans becoming the accessories. In a very real sense, as computing power tends to infinity the need for human ingenuity (in the design of efficient algorithms, for example) may approach zero. This is certainly true for many optimization problems: given enough computing speed, a dumb, case-by-case search for the optimal solution becomes a feasible option, even if there is an astronomical number of possibilities.

In a recent essay, the French mathematician René Thom denounced the failure of scientific theories to explain reality. "Scientists wanted to rid the ancients' universe of its magical and metaphysical entities," he wrote, "but they have themselves gradually introduced a myriad of objects and structures which cannot be observed, are increasingly difficult to imagine and practically no one understands."[3] In Thom's view, technological progress only masks the stagnation of our global understanding of the world. "Instead of helping us to understand, scientists are busy calculating, keeping their computers running," complained the 1958 winner of the prestigious Fields Medal—the mathematicians' Nobel Prize. "Science has become a huge collection of recipes that work."

It may be all right for philosophers, in their perpetual search for explanations and ultimate causes, to spurn the merely pragmatic products of science and technology. But people whose main business is to solve practical problems are quite comfortable with "recipes" that get the job done.

Soft Solutions

Whether machines could one day take over problem-solving altogether is not the question, for computer output per se is meaningless without humans to make sense of the answers—and to ask the questions in the first place. What we are witnessing is rather the emergence of some original ways of circumventing the shortcomings of classical computation. Digital computers operate in a sequential, exact, and deterministic way on binary code. But such a mode of operation has its limits, both theoretical and practical, and so there are problems that digital computers cannot solve. Another limitation of conventional computers is the requirement that they be provided with a program. Some of the new computing paradigms, on the other hand, make room for devices that do not have to be programmed in the traditional sense but can "learn" by experience, much as our own brain does.

Interest in the new ideas also stems from a desire to build "intelligent" machines, with humanlike capabilities of cognition and decision making. (Unfortunately, the qualifier "intelligent" has been so abused lately that it has become practically meaningless. We have intelligent chips, intelligent doors, intelligent cars, etc. What label will be used for the next generation of gadgets?) In this respect, digital computers may fail miserably. Even if the computer can play chess and beat the best human players, its strategy is far from clever. It is essentially a brute force technique based on decision trees representing millions of possibilities, and from which the optimal move is chosen. The human player takes a more "intelligent"—if inscrutable

—approach, since the brain cannot anticipate the consequences of more than a few moves at a time.

For Lotfi Zadeh, who invented fuzzy sets (the subject of chapter 1), the difference between human and machine intelligence lies in the ability of the human brain to think and reason in imprecise, nonquantitative terms, an ability that present-day digital computers do not possess. According to Zadeh, "It is this ability that makes it possible for humans to decipher sloppy hand-writing, understand distorted speech, and focus on that information that is relevant to a decision. It is the lack of this ability that makes even the most sophisticated large-scale computer incapable of communicating with humans in natural—rather than artificially constructed—languages."[4] If we are to build machines that "reason" more like humans, we must look beyond the classical Von Neumann computer.

Fuzzy logic, neural networks, and genetic algorithms are among the most successful novel approaches to computation and problem-solving. Neural networks can recognize ill-defined patterns without an explicit set of rules; fuzzy logic controls systems from a partial and imprecise description of their behavior; and genetic algorithms can solve complex problems by an "evolutionary" process in which chance plays a fundamental role. These techniques, which should be seen as complementary rather than competitive, are at the core of the "soft computing" approach to machine intelligence. Some of its principal traits are uncertain, ambiguous, or incomplete data; massive parallelism; randomness; approximate solutions, and self-modifying programs.

Even more profound mutations may be in store. In 1994, Leonard Adleman demonstrated the feasibility of carrying out computations at the molecular level. "One can imagine," he wrote at the end of his paper,[5] "the eventual emergence of a general purpose computer consisting of nothing more than a single macromolecule conjugated to a ribosomelike collection of enzymes that act on it." Although still only a theoretical possibility, quantum computers (devices that use the polarization of photons to encode information) might force us one day to redefine what we mean by a computation.

It must be emphasized, though, that digital computers, which are extremely fast and precise for executing certain tasks—performing sequences of arithmetical operations, for instance—will not soon become a thing of the past. The new technology tends to complement rather than replace them. Furthermore, the novel modes of computation—fuzzy, neural, genetic—are for now mostly implemented on conventional computers.

About the Book

> Where computers race for faster calculations,
> mathematics races for more clever algorithms. An idea
> that cuts in half the number of steps is as good as a chip
> that doubles the speed.
> *(MIT mathematician Gilbert Strang)*[6]

This book presents the principles of soft computing in a short, direct fashion. I have tried to make the basic concepts accessible to a broad audience, without the technical clutter but beyond the simple metaphors, occasionally also casting a critical eye on the subject matter. My chief goal has been to expose, in an entertaining though rigorous way, the (mostly mathematical) ideas behind fuzzy logic, neural networks, and genetic algorithms, too often obscured by the suggestive terminology (neurons, learning, chromosomes, etc.) used by the practitioners in these fields. This is done in parts 1 and 3.

The new ideas can only be fully appreciated against the background of traditional—"hard"—computing and its mathematical underpinning. From Turing machines to NP-complete problems, chapter 3 is a tour of the concepts at the heart of classical computing designed to give the reader a proper perspective, with an emphasis on the limitations of the traditional modes of calculation. Chapter 4 focuses on the foundations of mathematics, in particular on the role of computers in the search for mathematical truth. After retelling an old but always captivating story (Gödel's Incompleteness Theorem), I explore the somewhat humbling prospect that some mathematical truths might not be verifiable by the human mind without the assistance of the computer.

Mathematics and computers complement each other; software/ hardware are two sides of the same coin. But too often people only marvel at the body of the machine—the magic of its chips and optical scanners, the dazzle of its animated 3D images—and forget (or never know) that its soul is mathematical. One of the aims of this book is to counterbalance that one-sided perception by giving proper credit to the invisible hand of mathematics.

NOTES

1. A. J. Marder, *From the Dreadnought to Scapa Flow*, OUP, Oxford, 1961–70, 5 vols.

2. Ted Gruetzner, as quoted in "Problem in Reactor May Be Widespread," *The Globe and Mail*, 10 January 1997.

3. René Thom, in *La Magie Contemporaine. L'Échec du savoir moderne*, pp. 19–35, Yvon Johannisse ed., Québec/Amérique, 1994.

4. *Fuzzy Sets: Theory and Applications to Policy Analysis and Information Systems*, Paul P. Wang and S. K. Chang, eds., Plenum Press, New York and London, p. 196 (1980).

5. Leonard M. Adleman, "Molecular Computation of Solutions to Combinatorial Problems," *Science*, vol. 266, 11 November 1994, pp. 1021–24.

6. Gilbert Strang, "Wavelets," *American Scientist*, vol. 82, May–June 1994, p. 255.

* *Acknowledgments* *

I WISH to express my recognition to several people who read parts of the manuscript and whose tactful criticism and/or (overstated?) praise helped me produce a better book: Peter Géczy, Toyohashi University of Technology, Japan; Michel Grabisch, Thomson-CSF Central Research Laboratory, Orsay, France; Kazuo Nakamura, Laboratory For International Fuzzy Engineering Research, Yokohama, Japan; Andrew Watson, Institute of Food Research, Norwich, U.K.; and Doron Zeilberger, Temple University, Philadelphia. Thank you Peter, Michel, Kazuo, Andrew, and Doron.

I am also indebted to the people at Princeton University Press who were involved in the production of this book, in particular to Bill Laznovsky, for his excellent copyediting and his attention to detail. Special thanks go to my editor, Trevor Lipscombe, for his patience, for his abundant and valuable comments, and for making it all happen.

ARTURO SANGALLI
Sherbrooke, Quebec
June 1998

* *To the Reader* *

T HE THREE PARTS are largely independent entities, and could be read in a different order without loss of continuity. Some mathematical proofs and technical details have been relegated to the appendices.

I have written this book with a large public in mind, ranging from the layperson to the expert, and assuming only a knowledge of elementary mathematical concepts. Familiarity with more advanced mathematics (such as vector algebra and differential calculus) might occasionally help, but a curious mind is really the only prerequisite for appreciating most of the text.

PART ONE

BLURRED VISIONS

*

CHAPTER ONE

Classes with Uncertain Borders

A MATHEMATICS OF CLOUDY QUANTITIES

Theoretical physics demands the highest possible standard of
rigorous precision in the description of relations, such as only
the use of mathematical language can give.
(Albert Einstein, on the structure of theoretical physics)[1]

IN THE OPENING sentence of a paper published in 1965,[2] Lotfi Zadeh
made a basic observation: most collections of objects we encounter in
the real world are not precisely defined. Zadeh, a professor of
electrical engineering at the University of California, cited as an
example the class of animals. Clearly, any dog, horse, or bird is in this
class, while rocks, fluids, and plants are not. But objects such as
starfish and bacteria have an ambiguous status; the contradictory
terms "animal" and "not animal" both seem to describe them to
some degree. Likewise, "round shapes," "old cars," and "low temperatures," do not admit a precise definition.

And yet, classes with uncertain borders pervade human language
and thinking and play an important role in the communication of
information. Zadeh's idea was to quantify this uncertainty, which is
due not to chance but to the absence of sharply defined criteria of
class membership. The resulting concept—that of a fuzzy set—uses
the rigorous precision of mathematics to manage the imprecision of
human expression and thought. If Zadeh's paper had begun by
stating the obvious, what followed was ground-breaking. This opening chapter is a guided tour of fuzzy sets and their offspring (fuzzy
logic).

SETS, LOGIC, AND BOOLEAN ALGEBRAS

Before we get to the notion of a fuzzy set, it is wise to spend some
time with ordinary sets. The two concepts are directly connected: the
familiar sets are special cases of fuzzy ones.

Once studied only by mathematicians and philosophers interested in the foundations of mathematics, sets are now taught in elementary school and even to toddlers in kindergarten—a relic of the "new math" revolution of the 1970s. But it is questionable whether such an early (and superficial) acquaintance with sets heightens the mathematical or logical skills of the student.

A set is usually conceived as "a collection of objects," but this description is not very enlightening. What matters is to be able to tell which objects are in the set and which ones are not. For instance, if Z denotes the set of all winners of the Nobel Prize in chemistry, then Ernest Rutherford, Marie Curie, and Ilya Prigogine are all in Z (they won the prestigious prize in 1908, 1911, and 1977, respectively). On the other hand, Frank Sinatra and Margaret Thatcher are not in Z—as of this writing. For a mathematical example, let P be the set of all prime numbers. Then 2, 7, and 13 are definitely in (or belong to, are elements/members of) P, while 10, 22, and 63 are out. For very large numbers the classification may take a while, but it is nonetheless clear-cut: n is in P if it is not divisible by any number smaller than itself—except, of course, the number 1.

P is a subset of the larger set N of all natural numbers—the numbers 0, 1, 2, 3,... and so on that we use for counting. We can conveniently represent membership in a subset as a binary digit: 1 for a member and 0 for a nonmember. The symbol $P(x)$ denotes the grade of membership of the natural number x in the subset P. For example, $P(7) = 1$, $P(15) = 0$, $P(2^{859,433}) = 0$ and $P(2^{859,433} - 1) = 1$. (According to the 1995 Guinness Book of Records, the number $2^{859,433} - 1$ is prime—but do not waste your time trying to check it out. It was found to be prime with the help of a supercomputer in January 1994 and at the time it was the largest known prime number. Just for the record, there is no such thing as *the* largest prime number.)

Sets may be combined in various ways to form other sets. Given two sets A and B, their union is the set $A \cup B$ consisting of those objects that are in either A or B. For example, if A is the set of divisors of 10 (i.e., $A = \{1, 2, 5, 10\}$) and B the set of divisors of 15 ($B = \{1, 3, 5, 15\}$), then $A \cup B = \{1, 2, 5, 10, 3, 15\}$—the set of numbers that divide either 10 or 15 (or both). The intersection $A \cap B$ is formed by the objects in both A and B. Referring to the above example, $A \cap B = \{1, 5\}$—the common divisors of 10 and 15.

Union and intersection may be visualized with the help of so-called Venn diagrams, in which sets are drawn as circles or other closed

4

curves. John Venn, a nineteenth-century English logician, is chiefly remembered for his use of such geometric diagrams to depict relations among sets. If for each set we draw a circle, then their union is represented by the region inside the circles, and their intersection by the region common to both circles (the shaded parts of figure I.1).

When we agree on the kind of objects we wish to talk about, we have a "universe of discourse" or universal set U. Then each set A has a complement $\overline{A}$, made up of the objects in U that are not members of A. For example, if we are discussing the natural numbers and A is the set of all even numbers $\{0, 2, 4, \ldots\}$, then $\overline{A}$ is the set of all odd numbers $\{1, 3, 5, \ldots\}$. Venn's treatment of U was criticized by C. L. Dodgson, a.k.a. Lewis Carroll. The author of *Alice in Wonderland*, better known for his literary than for his mathematical achievements, insisted on the need to enclose the circles by a rectangle, thus delimiting the universe of discourse. In this way, the complement of A is represented by the region outside the circle but inside the rectangle (fig. I.2).

The three operations introduced above are particular ways of combining subsets (of a given set) to form other subsets. Repeated combinations, represented by expressions such as $(A \cap \overline{B}) \cup (\overline{A \cup C})$ give rise to an "algebra" first studied by the British mathematician George Boole and later named after him. The structure of this Boolean algebra of classes mirrors that of the algebra of logic that Boole invented in the 1850s. His idea was to replace the usual process of

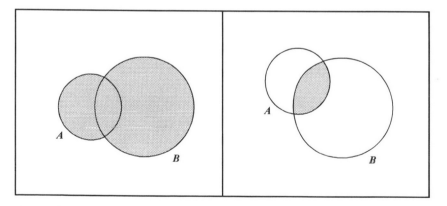

FIGURE I.1. Venn diagrams representing the union (*left*) and the intersection (*right*) of sets A and B.

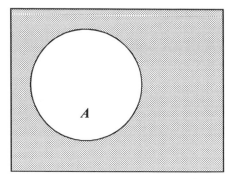

FIGURE I.2. A Venn diagram of the complement of the set A.

logical deduction by the algebraic manipulation of formal expressions. In Boole's propositional calculus, letters represent statements that can be combined using the connectives "or," "&," and "not"—the linguistic counterparts of the set-operations of union, intersection, and complement, respectively.

Technical applications of Boole's algebra of logic had to wait almost a century. In 1938, Claude E. Shannon, who would later become famous for his mathematical theory of communication, was a graduate student at the Massachusetts Institute of Technology. In his Master's thesis, Shannon showed how Boolean algebras could be used in the analysis and design of electrical circuits.[3] Made up of relay contacts and switches connected in series or in parallel, these circuits occurred in automatic telephone exchanges and in the control of industrial motors. Similar circuits, built from elements called logic gates, perform operations on binary signals and constitute today the central nervous system of electronic digital computers.

Underlying the practical applications of Boolean algebras—to propositional logic, circuits, digital computers, and so on—there is an elegant mathematical theory: the symbolic calculus of binary functions of n binary variables. Modern scientists and engineers could take this theoretical tool for granted thanks to Boole's genial demonstration that reasoning could be performed by "calculating" or, to put it bluntly, that logic could be reduced to algebra.

FUZZY SETS

What characterizes a set is the necessity, for any given object, to be or not to be in the set. While this dichotomy *à la* Hamlet works well for mathematical objects such as numbers, when we try to apply it to the real world we realize that there is a problem. Surely, some objects can be classified without hesitation: a dog is an animal and a banana is not. Pianist Artur Rubinstein was definitely old when he died in 1982 (he was 95), and Mozart, a child prodigy, was certainly not old when he composed his first sonata (at age 7). But was the colorful Picasso old when he painted *Portrait of Dora Maar* (he was 56)? Are sponges animals?

The class of aquatic animals and the class of old persons are not sets in the ordinary sense because neither "aquatic animal" nor "old person" are well-defined concepts. To deal with such ill-defined classes, Zadeh's idea was to allow the grade of membership to be any number between 0 and 1. He called these classes *fuzzy sets*. Zadeh expected this new concept, which generalized that of an ordinary set, to have applications in the fields of pattern recognition and the communication of information. The future would prove him right, but it would also prove that he had largely underestimated the potential of his creation.

Unlike the borders of ordinary sets, those of fuzzy sets are not sharp but, well...fuzzy. And because fuzzy sets make room for partial membership, that is, for objects that are neither totally in nor totally out, they can accommodate better than ordinary sets the ambiguity of human language. Take the class of old persons, for instance. At age 5, a person is definitely not old (grade of membership 0) and at age 95, the person is clearly old (grade of membership 1). But somewhere between 5 and 95 there is a gray zone, represented numerically by membership grades greater than 0 and less than 1. For example, a 40-year-old person may have grade of membership 0.30 in the fuzzy set of old persons (intuitively: the description of such a person as "old" is 30 percent accurate). At age 58, the membership grade may attain 0.70 or 0.75, and it will be 1 by the time the person has reached age 85.

The important point here is that there is no sharp borderline, no magic age g such that you become old (and stay so) the moment you reach it—but you were not old the previous day. This situation is not due to our incomplete knowledge or to our inability to calculate g. It is due to the fact that "old" cannot be captured in one precise definition the way "prime number" or "Nobel laureate" can. Of course, one can always proclaim that "old person" means "age equal to or greater than 65 years." While such an arbitrary definition may be convenient for some purposes, the class it characterizes is fundamentally different from the class of old persons: the former is an ordinary set, the latter is not.

Another example of a fuzzy set is the class P of poor people. We shall see that treating P as a well-defined set leads to an absurdity. For if someone with a certain annual income X ($2,000, say) is a member of P, then so is a person whose annual income is $X + 1$ (certainly one more dollar per year cannot prevent indigence). For the same reason, those with incomes of $X + 2$, $X + 3$, and so on, are also poor. But then, by repeating this argument enough times we would eventually conclude that an individual making $100,000 a year is poor! This paradox can be explained by assuming the existence of a "poverty line," so dear to government statisticians, for in that case the dollar that allows you to cross the line does make a difference—which only confirms what common sense suggests: that the official notion of poor is different from the natural one.

It is important to realize that the concept of a fuzzy set is not statistical in nature, that there is a difference between fuzziness and randomness. Fuzziness in Zadeh's sense represents vagueness due to human intuition, not probability. Probability has to do with the occurrence of events, and when all the facts are in, a given event either has occurred or it has not. The sum of the two dice we rolled is or is not 7; when the roulette wheel stops, the compartment containing the ball is black or not. But questions such as: Was the talk long? Was the speaker short? Was the conference room big? cannot always be answered by yes or no, even after all the facts (the length of the talk, the speaker's height, and the dimensions of the room) are in.

Certain fuzzy sets, especially fuzzy subsets of numbers, can be visualized by depicting them as in figure I.3. In mathematical terms, these are simply the usual graphs of the membership functions $y = A(x)$ in a Cartesian coordinate system. These graphs are frequently either triangular or trapezoidal and, occasionally, bell-shaped or of some other form. The simpler shapes are preferred because they make number crunching easier.

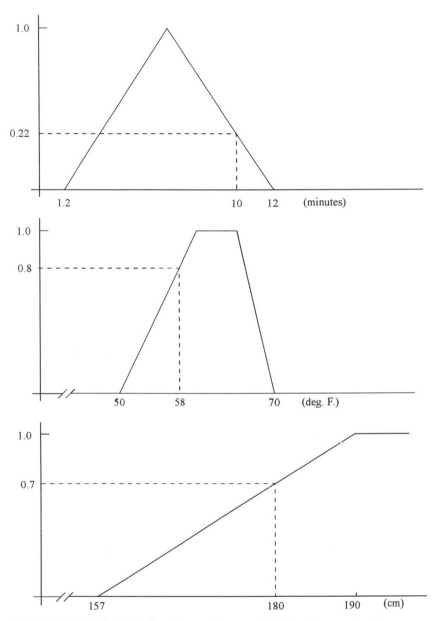

FIGURE I.3. Membership functions of fuzzy sets. *Top*: Fuzzy set of average washing times for a washing machine. For example: 10 (minutes) has a grade of membership of 0.22 in this fuzzy set. *Center*: Fuzzy set of cool temperatures. *Bottom*: Fuzzy set of tall persons.

It must be emphasized that it is one thing to conceive a given class A as a fuzzy set and another, quite different thing, to be able to specify its membership function $A(x)$. Just as there is no "poverty line," sharply separating the poor from the nonpoor, there is no such thing as the true membership function for the fuzzy set of poor people, or for any other fuzzy set. This is not to say that the choice of the membership grades is completely arbitrary. Both theoretical and empirical considerations intervene in the selection, as do the context and the particular situation to be modeled. The increasing use of learning and optimization techniques, such as neural networks and genetic algorithms, is gradually rendering the selection of member- ship functions less of an art and more of a science. But regardless of the method employed (educated guess or algorithm), in the practical applications of fuzzy sets the main reason for choosing a particular membership function is ultimately "because it works."

Graphs such as those in figure I.3 are a convenient way of repre- senting single fuzzy subsets. To get a picture of the totality of fuzzy subsets (of some universal set X), there is a better technique. It was Bart Kosko's idea to represent each fuzzy subset of X by a point in a Cartesian coordinate system.[4] Suppose, for simplicity, that the uni- verse X consists of only two elements, $X = \{x_1, x_2\}$. Then, the fuzzy subset S of X in which x_1 has grade of membership 0.2 and x_2 has grade of membership 0.7, is represented by the point with coordi- nates $(0.2, 0.7)$ (figure I.4). In general, the fuzzy subset A of X is represented as the point with coordinates $(A(x_1), A(x_2))$.

Notice that this universe X has four ordinary subsets (which are of course special cases of fuzzy ones): $\{x_1, x_2\}, \{x_1\}, \{x_2\}$ and the empty subset $\{ \}$. The four vertices of the square then correspond to the ordinary subsets of X (e.g., $(0, 1)$ corresponds to $\{x_2\}$ and $(0, 0)$ to the empty subset). Going from the ordinary subsets to all the fuzzy subsets of X amounts to "filling up the square." It also means moving from the discrete (four points) to the continuum (the full square)—a vivid illustration of the abundance of fuzzy subsets.

The sets-as-points representation can be extended to higher dimen- sions. If $X = \{x_1, x_2, x_3\}$, the ordinary subsets of X are represented by the eight vertices of a cube in a three-dimensional Cartesian coordinate system, and the collection of all fuzzy subsets of X fills up the entire cube. The fuzzy subsets of an infinite X may be pictured as the points of an infinite-dimensional "hypercube."

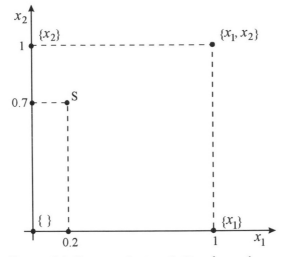

FIGURE I.4. Fuzzy subsets of $X = \{x_1, x_2\}$ as points of the unit square. The vertices of the square correspond to the four ordinary subsets of X. The point $(0.2, 0.7)$ represents a fuzzy subset S. The membership grades of x_1 and x_2 in S are 0.2 and 0.7, respectively.

OPERATIONS ON FUZZY SETS

Let us go back briefly to ordinary sets. If A and B are such (ordinary) sets, A is said to be *included* in B if every element of A is also an element of B. In symbols: $A \subseteq B$. For instance, the set of prime numbers greater than 2 is included in the set of odd numbers—this is the translation into set jargon of the fact that all primes greater than 2 are odd. The notion of set inclusion can be expressed using membership functions, for we have $A \subseteq B$ precisely if

$$\text{for all } x \text{ in the universal set, } A(x) \leq B(x). \tag{1}$$

In other words, $A \subseteq B$ means that given any x, its grade of membership in A cannot exceed its grade of membership in B—in crude terms, $A \subseteq B$ if no x can be in A "more" than it is in B. Since statement (1) is couched in the language of membership functions, it makes sense for all—fuzzy as well as ordinary—subsets of X. Thus,

11

we will say that the fuzzy subset A is included in the fuzzy subset B if (1) holds.

A similar approach can be used to extend the set operations (union, intersection, etc.) to fuzzy sets in a natural way. We first notice that the grade of membership of x in $A \cup B$ is the greatest (or maximum) of the two grades $A(x)$, $B(x)$. In symbols

$$(A \cup B)(x) = \max\{A(x), B(x)\}. \tag{2}$$

Likewise, the grade of membership of x in $A \cap B$, being the smallest (or minimum) of $A(x)$, $B(x)$, is given by the formula

$$(A \cap B)(x) = \min\{A(x), B(x)\}. \tag{3}$$

As for the membership grade of x in the complement $\overline{A}$, it follows from the equation

$$\overline{A}(x) = 1 - A(x) \tag{4}$$

(if x is in A, $\overline{A}(x) = 0$; if x is not in A, then $\overline{A}(x) = 1$).

The above three equations still make sense when $A(x)$ and $B(x)$ are numbers between 0 and 1, so they can be used to define "fuzzy" operations on fuzzy subsets. Equation (2), for instance, stipulates that the membership grade of x in the (fuzzy) union $A \cup B$ should be the largest of the two grades $A(x)$, $B(x)$. Figure I.5 illustrates the effect of these fuzzy operations on the graphs of membership functions.

Because the same rules of combination are used, the fuzzy union (or intersection) of two ordinary sets coincides with their usual union (intersection). In technical jargon, this fact is expressed by saying that the fuzzy operations are *extensions* of the familiar ones to the larger domain of all fuzzy subsets of X. But so are infinitely many other possible combinations of fuzzy subsets. For example, one can construct a new fuzzy subset C out of A and B by stipulating that

$$C(x) = A(x) + B(x) - A(x)B(x). \tag{5}$$

Then, a simple calculation confirms that if A and B are ordinary sets (i.e., $A(x)$ and $B(x)$ are restricted to being either 0 or 1), then C is their usual union. Although many other ways of combining two or more fuzzy subsets have been proposed, only a handful of them proved to have more than a purely theoretical interest.

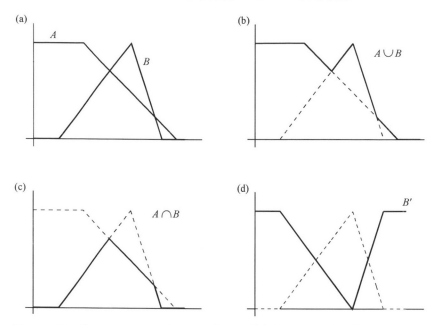

FIGURE I.5. Operations on fuzzy subsets. (*a*) Membership functions of the fuzzy subsets *A* and *B*. (*b*) Membership function of their union; (*c*) of their intersection; and (*d*) of the complement of *B*.

FUZZINESS AS MULTI-VALUED LOGIC

The membership grade $A(x)$ of x in the fuzzy set A is usually seen as measuring "to what extent" x is in A. But $A(x)$ may also be interpreted as the degree of truth of the statement "x is in A." For an ordinary set, $A(x)$ is either 1 or 0, depending on whether the statement "x is in A" is true or false. But if A is fuzzy, the truth-value of "x is in A" can be any number between 0 and 1. Take A to be the fuzzy set of expensive cars, for instance. If c is a given car, then $A(c)$ represents the degree to which the statement "car c is expensive" is true. Such "fuzzy" statements extend the traditional, two-valued logic by allowing for a continuum of shades of truth.

Here is another example. In 1991, Hitachi built a prototype of a security device (actually a neural network) that can be trained to recognize signatures. You have first to provide three samples of your signature by signing with a special pen on an electronic pad. Interest-

13

ingly, the machine will record not only your signature as a graphical object, but also the pace at which you traced it out (more precisely, the vertical and horizontal components of the velocity vector associated with the tip of the pen). Anyone trying to fool the machine would then have to forge your signature by writing it out at the same speed as you normally do. To have your signature validated, you sign again on the pad, this time with the machine on "verify" mode. After a short interval, the screen will display a number between 0 and 1. If this number is, say, 0.93, then the match between your present sample and the original signature is 93 percent. This might be interpreted as meaning that the statement "the person who has just signed is Sandra Smith" has a truth value equal to 0.93—not absolutely true but probably close enough to authorize the withdrawal of $100,000 from Ms. Smith's bank account.

PRECISION

All traditional logic assumes that precise symbols are
being employed. It is therefore not applicable to this
terrestrial life, but only to an imaginary celestial existence.
(Bertrand Russell)[5]

In the ideal realm of mathematics, things are certain and precise. But in the real world, absolute precision and certitude are very rare commodities. The ratio of the circumference of the circle to its diameter is exactly π, but in our practical calculations we must do with a decimal approximation. The heights of a perfect triangle meet at precisely one point—but real triangles are never perfect and points exist only in our imagination. While mathematical statements are either true or false, such strict dichotomy fails for assertions in our everyday life, which is seldom—if ever—black or white.

Digital clocks, speedometers, and pocket calculators flash out numerals with liquid-crystal clarity. But how significant are those figures and how much precision do we really need in our daily life? Imprecise concepts (love, justice, bad, nice, big, funny) pervade our thoughts and our speech. The jurors' interpretation of such a nebu-

14

lous notion as "reasonable doubt" can be, for some, a matter of life or death.

Philosophy's eternal quest for knowledge and wisdom is couched in human—hence, inexact—language. Massachusetts Institute of Technology mathematician Gian-Carlo Rota condemns contemporary philosophers who, in their attempts to imitate mathematics, approach philosophical questions with what he calls "the myth of precision."[6] He notes that a concept need not be rigorously precise to be meaningful. "Our everyday reasoning is not precise," says Rota, "but it is nevertheless efficient. Nature itself, from galaxies to genes, is approximate and inexact." And he adds, "Philosophical concepts are among the least precise. Terms such as 'mind,' 'perception,' 'memory,' and 'knowledge' do not have either a fixed nor a clear meaning but they make sense just the same."

Quantifying a phenomenon in a seemingly accurate way makes it appear to be exact and well understood. During a lecture in Japan, Lotfi Zadeh once quoted a newspaper article according to which the probability of a tremor of degree 6 on the seismic scale occurring within two months was 11 percent. "Readers of this article," he observed, "would gain the wrong impression that the figure of 11 percent, instead of 10 or 12 percent, is concluded because of sufficient knowledge about earthquakes."

According to Zadeh, complexity and precision bear an inverse relation to each other, for as the complexity of a problem increases, the possibility of analyzing it in precise terms diminishes. And so, some "fuzzy thinking" may be legitimate, if it makes possible the solution of problems which are much too complex for accurate analysis.

In many situations, precision may be costly or take too much time. Zadeh gives as a simple example the ordinary task of parking a car. "Usually, a driver can park a car without too much difficulty, because the final position of the car is not specified exactly. If it were specified with high precision, it would take days and perhaps months to park the car."[7] A more sophisticated example is the coding of (digitized) television images by data compression techniques. The loss of some precision in the reconstructed image, hardly perceptible to the human eye, is largely compensated by the increased speed of transmission. It is this tolerance for imprecision that fuzzy logic exploits in many of its applications.

What Is Fuzzy Logic?

Consumers generally blame themselves for their inability to use machines, from VCRs and electronic ovens to personal computers. But is it their fault if they cannot think like the machine—a talent that most designers of machines seem to take for granted? A general goal of fuzzy logic is to help build machines that reason more like humans, so that humans should not need to think like machines.

The expression "fuzzy logic" sounds like a contradiction in terms, and it would hardly be taken as a compliment to be told that one's logic is "fuzzy." In its original and technical sense, fuzzy logic is a mathematical method, based on the theory of fuzzy sets, that helps machines to "reason" more like humans. Fuzzy logic is usually implemented by an algorithm, or program, for a conventional digital computer and, as such, it is exact. But the method has also a subjective component—hence, essentially empirical and inexact—for it presupposes the translation in numerical form of the vagueness of human language and knowledge.

This duality—exact/inexact—of fuzzy logic, which I believe is one of its strengths, is also a source of misunderstanding. Many critics, bona fide or otherwise, of fuzzy logic focus on only one of the aspects. "Fuzzy logic is claimed to use vague concepts and imprecise data. This is false," wrote an unhappy reader of one of my popularization articles.[8] And he or she—I could not tell from the initials— went on: "Fuzzy logic takes precise, analogue inputs, does some fancy processing, then produces precise analogue outputs. I call this analogue signal processing." The reader is basically right, but he or she omits to acknowledge the role of fuzzy logic in devising that "fancy processing."

At the other extreme there are those who criticize the imprecise side of fuzzy logic. Here is an excerpt from another letter: "Of course, simplistic thinking may be adequate in simple cases, and fuzzy logic may indeed be capable of scheduling elevators and washing machines. But so are probabilistic arguments. The real danger with inconsistent, faddish reasoning would come if it were ever applied to important matters like air safety or reactor control. Fuzzy thinking about such matters would be dangerous as well as deplorable."

Such a reaction is typical of people who regard fuzzy logic, not just as a specific method (algorithm) but as a general attitude or philosophy. This philosophy of fuzziness has both its detractors and its followers. When applied to the solution of practical problems, the fuzzy approach is, for its detractors, at best redundant and at worst irresponsible and dangerous. "If it's fuzzy, it can't be serious" could well be their motto.

For the believers, on the other hand, fuzzy thinking is a powerful way to understand human reasoning and to deal with the complexity of the real world. Nowhere has this fascination with fuzziness been more manifest than in Japan. "Fuzziness is inherent in the Japanese culture," says Toshiro Terano, director of the Laboratory for Fuzzy Engineering Research (LIFE) in Yokohama. And so it may not be accidental that Japanese scientists and engineers should play such a key role in developing the practical applications that made fuzzy logic popular. Terano sees fuzzy logic both as a tool and as a new paradigm for solving problems for which exact mathematical models are difficult or impossible to obtain. "As a tool, fuzzy logic can capture the uncertain meaning of words and treat the subjectivity and intuition of the human thinking process," he observes.

The final word goes to Lotfi Zadeh, the creator of the concept. In the spring of 1994, Zadeh wrote: "The term fuzzy logic is actually used in two different senses. In a narrow sense, fuzzy logic is a logical system which is an extension of multivalued logic and is intended to serve as a logic of approximate reasoning. But in a wider sense, fuzzy logic is more or less synonymous with the theory of fuzzy sets, that is, a theory of classes with unsharp boundaries. What is important to recognize is that today the term fuzzy logic is used predominantly in its wider sense."[9]

However, Zadeh himself recently admitted that the term fuzzy logic may be misleading. Addressing an international meeting of experts at the University of California at Berkeley in the spring of 1996, he said: "In the things we are doing today [in fuzzy logic] we are not really dealing with logic. We are using mathematics, function manipulation and evaluation; strictly speaking, no logic, merely computation."[10] Such a clarification might help readers with a question most of them are likely to ask themselves sooner or later: This is fuzzy all right, but is it logic?

NOTES

1. A. Einstein, "Prinzipien der Forschung, Rede zur 60. Geburstag von Max Planck" (1918), in *Mein Weltbild*, Ullstein Verlag, 1977, pp. 108–9, trans. *Ideas and Opinions* (New York: Crown, 1954), pp. 225–26. As quoted in *Order Out of Chaos*, I. Prigogine and Isabelle Stengers, Flamingo (Fontana Paperbacks), 1985, pp. 52–53.

2. L. A. Zadeh, "Fuzzy Sets," *Information and Control* 8, 338–56 (1965).

3. Claude E. Shannon, "A Symbolic Analysis of Relay and Switching Circuits," *AIEE Transactions*, vol. 57, pp. 713–23, 1938.

4. B. Kosko, "Fuzziness vs. Probability," *International Journal of General Systems*, vol. 17, nos. 2–3, Gordon and Breach Science Publishers, 1990.

5. B. Russell, "Vagueness," *Australian J. Phil.* 1, 84–92 (1923).

6. G.-C. Rota, "The Pernicious Influence of Mathematics upon Philosophy," *Synthese 88*, 1991.

7. L. A. Zadeh, "The Calculus of Fuzzy If/Then Rules," *AI Expert*, vol. 7, no. 3, March 1992, 23–27.

8. A. Sangalli, "Fuzzy Logic Goes to Market," *New Scientist*, vol. 133, no. 1807, 8 February 1992, pp. 36–39.

9. L. A. Zadeh, "Fuzzy Logic and Soft Computing: Issues, Contentions and Perspectives," *Proceedings of the 3rd International Conference on Fuzzy Logic, Neural Nets and Soft Computing* (Iizuka, Japan, August 1–7, 1994), pp. 1–2.

10. 1996 Biennial Conference of the North American Fuzzy Information Processing Association NAFIPS (University of California at Berkeley, June 19–22, 1996), plenary talk.

CHAPTER TWO

Fuzzy Does It

A SIMPLE CONTROL PROBLEM

*It is not always necessary to understand a system in order to
control it. Is there a better example of this principle's
plausibility than our own brain? After all, human beings
have used it for thousands of years without having the
slightest idea of how it worked.*

Suppose you are driving on the highway. Realizing that the gap
between your car and the vehicle ahead is closing, you put on the
brakes. The amount of pressure you apply on the pedal depends on
several factors: the speed of your car, the distance separating the two
vehicles, how fast is this distance decreasing, road conditions, and so
on. But you do not need to know the numerical values of these
quantities in order to "deduce" the adequate braking pressure. As an
experienced driver, you put the right pressure on the brake pedal
instinctively, you have developed a feeling for it. Fuzzy logic is a
method for transmitting that same "feeling" to a machine, a procedure that allows the easy encoding of human know-how in a form
computers can understand and use.

In technical jargon, the above highway situation translates as follows. Your car and the vehicle ahead of you form a system. Your
brain is acting as a controller of the distance between the two
vehicles. The goal of the control actions is to avoid collision by
keeping a safe distance. This analysis is useful if we are contemplat-
ing designing a machine to control the brakes automatically. The
device we have in mind would be fed all the relevant data (or input):
the speed of your car, the distance separating the two vehicles, and so
forth. From this information, it will be expected to calculate the
appropriate braking (output). Since the input data is continually
changing, the input/output cycle should take place at regular intervals (perhaps many times per second) to ensure proper control.

We have here what engineers call a control problem: from the values of some input variables (speed, distance, etc.) calculate the value of the output variable (pressure on the brake pedal) that guarantees a satisfactory performance of the system (safe driving distance).

The classical approach for solving this problem requires a mathematical model of the system. This is typically a set of differential equations relating the numerical quantities involved and their rates of change. The appropriate braking pressure then results from solving the equations. Summing up, our control problem will be solved, in theory at least, if we can come up with: (*a*) a mathematical description of the system and (*b*) a method for solving the equations arising in part (*a*) in real time (this last condition is crucial, for the controller should be able to take action before it is too late to avoid a collision). This is the conventional solution scheme.

Some twenty years ago a different approach was tried for the first time. Based on the theory of fuzzy sets, the new technique bypasses requirement (*a*)—the need for a mathematical model. Instead, its central idea is to encode a linguistic version of the operations required to control the system.

To apply the new method to our braking problem, we must begin with an analysis of the actions the driver takes, that is, how the driver responds, by braking, to the various speed and distance conditions. This human expertise is then put in the form of conditional rules:

If (PRESENT CONDITIONS), then (ACTION TO BE TAKEN).

The charm of it is that these rules may be phrased using the "fuzzy" notions of everyday language. For example: "If your speed is medium and the distance to the vehicle ahead is safe and it is decreasing rather fast, then apply a moderate pressure on the brake."

In order to treat this information numerically, the imprecise expressions "safe distance," "moderate pressure," and so forth are represented mathematically as fuzzy sets. Then, the operating rules are encoded into a program for the computer or fuzzy controller. While you drive on the highway, sensors will measure the input data (speed, distance, etc.) and pass this information on to the fuzzy controller. Using an algorithm known as fuzzy inference, the controller will then calculate the correct pressure on the brake. If all goes well, your car (and yourself) will reach its destination in one piece.

This example, although somewhat artificial, serves to illustrate the concepts involved in a control problem and the general idea of a fuzzy logic solution. A fuzzy controller based essentially on the same principles has been tested by the French automobile manufacturer Peugeot.[1] The experimental car is equipped with a safety feature capable of taking over braking in case the driver is suddenly distracted or disabled. Using four input variables and twenty operating rules, the controller calculates the braking pressure in an emergency.

Commercial applications of fuzzy control by the car industry are already available to consumers—who will not necessarily notice it. Several Japanese manufacturers use fuzzy logic to control the automatic transmission of their models. The cruise control system of the 1994 Mazda Sentia employs fuzzy logic to prevent shifting to a higher gear during uphill driving,[2] and in the 1998 Volkswagen New Beetle fuzzy logic adapts the automatic transmission to the driver's style.

ORIGINS OF FUZZY CONTROL

Retracing the origins of an idea (who did what and—especially—when) is always a delicate question, but it seems safe to give credit to Abe Mamdani for the first demonstration of the practical possibilities of fuzzy set theory. Mamdani was a lecturer in the Department of Electrical Engineering at Queen Mary College (now Queen Mary and Westfield), in London, in the early 1970s, when he and his student Seto Assilian used fuzzy logic to control the operation of a small steam engine.[3] Fuzzy process control was born.

In retrospect, it was the implementation of a simple idea: automating the decisions a human expert makes to control a process. One of the earliest works in this direction uses the expert's knowledge put in the form of linguistic rules. It is due to D. A. Watermann, who investigated automatic learning in connection with the game of poker.[4] Mamdani acknowledges its influence on the development of the new technique. "In fact," he writes "it should be remarked that the work on process control using fuzzy logic was inspired as much by Watermann and his approach to rule-based decision making as by Zadeh and his novel theory of fuzzy subsets."[5]

Conventional control engineering is based on explicit mathematical models. This approach is successful when the models can be given as simple (in general, linear) differential equations relating a small number of input and output variables. But many processes, such as complex chemical reactions or the operation of an industrial plant, do not yield to such an approach because nobody actually understands how they work. The number of variables involved in those processes makes it impossible to specify all their complex interrelations with mathematical precision. In such cases, resorting to fuzzy logic is appealing because the design of a "fuzzy" controller does not require an exact theoretical model. It is enough to have a general strategy for controlling the process, such as the knowledge of an experienced operator.

Once the efficiency of Mamdani's method had been experimentally established, many others took up the idea of using fuzzy logic in process control; from industrial processes, such as cement manufacture, water purification, and the automatic operation of a subway train, to household appliances.

In 1980, the Danish cement manufacturer F. L. Smidth & Co. A/S used a fuzzy controller to regulate the operation of a cement kiln. This was the world's first industrial implementation of fuzzy logic techniques. A cement kiln is a rotating chamber where limestone, clay, sand, and iron ore are burned at high temperatures. The small nuts of minerals formed in the process are later ground down into cement. The process is controlled by varying the kiln rotational speed, the fuel rate, and the speed of the induction fan that sucks the hot combustion gases. An exact model is not feasible because the kiln is subject to random disturbances which cannot be quantified and its response to the operator's actions is extremely variable.

Three years later, in 1983, the water purification plant of Akita City in Japan employed fuzzy techniques developed by Fuji Electric Co. Ltd. to control the injection of chemicals. The decade's most spectacular application of fuzzy logic was the fuzzy predictive system that to this day operates the automated subway trains in the Japanese city of Sendai.[6] Braking and acceleration are reportedly smoother than in manually operated trains, making for a more comfortable and safer ride for passengers. The system, designed by Hitachi's engineers, has reduced energy consumption by 10 percent. It has also lowered the margin of error in stopping the trains at specified targets in stations to less than 10 cm—better than most veteran drivers, according to an official of the Municipal Transportation Bureau.

Similar techniques would later be incorporated in expert systems and spread to fields as diverse as medical diagnosis, image understanding by robots, and the forecasting of currency exchange rates. We shall discuss applications in a later section. For now, let us take a closer look at the technique itself.

COMPUTING WITH WORDS

For the famous astronomer Galileo and many of his successors, the Book of Nature was written in the language of mathematics, "and its characters are triangles, circles and other geometric figures." We know today that such an idealistic expectation, based more on faith than on fact, is only partially true, even if mathematics has considerably grown since Galileo's time. Of course, many observed or theoretical relationships can be condensed in a precise mathematical formula. A famous example is Einstein's $E = mc^2$, relating energy, mass, and the speed of light. But other relationships are imperfectly known, and can at best be described in the vague terms of natural language

if x is small and y is average, then z is large.

In cases like this we say that x, y, and z are "linguistic" variables, because their values are not numbers but words (small, large, etc.). Using fuzzy sets, we can turn these words into numerical relations on which calculations can be performed. Such is the power of fuzzy logic, which Lotfi Zadeh once called "a method for computing with words."

The values of a linguistic variable x are actually fuzzy subsets of some set X of numbers. For example, let x represent the speed of a car (in kilometers per hour) and let its linguistic values be "small," "average," and "high." Then X could be the set of numbers from 0 to 200, and each of those three words would then name some fuzzy subset of X.

A fuzzy inference rule has the general form

$$\text{if } x \text{ is } A \text{ and } y \text{ is } B \text{ then } z \text{ is } C \qquad (6)$$

23

where A, B, and C are words naming fuzzy subsets. In practical applications to control, (6) describes a relationship between the input variables (x and y) and the required control action (the output variable z). For example, "if temperature (x) is high (A) and image density (y) is low (B), then charge (z) is high (C)," is one of the nine rules that control the amount of electrical charge that should be imparted to the drum of a photocopying machine. The charge (z) depends on the temperature (x) and on the density, or black/white ratio (y) of the image being copied.

A BALANCING ACT OF CONTROL

To balance a stick on the palm of one hand is almost child's play. But how do we teach a robot to do the trick? The story of Takeshi Yamakawa's answer to this question provides a remarkable insight into the methodology and the power of fuzzy control. At the time, in 1987, he was in the Department of Electrical Engineering and Computer Science at Kumamoto University, but shortly after he joined the newly founded Kyushu Institute of Technology in Iizuka. Both institutions are located in the Western Japanese island of Kyushu.

Yamakawa's system[7] consists of a small vehicle (the "robot's hand") with a rigid pole (the "stick") joined to it by a pivot, as shown in figure I.6. The vehicle, driven by a servo motor, can move back and forth along a rectilinear track. To balance the pole, this motion must take place at an appropriate speed that is constantly changing.

We can derive a mathematical model of the problem from the laws of physics. The relevant time-dependent variables are the position of the vehicle along the track (y); the angle formed by the pole with the vertical (θ) and their rates of change with respect to time or, in mathematical terms, their derivatives: y' (velocity of the vehicle), y'' (its acceleration), θ' (angular velocity of the pole), and θ'' (angular acceleration); the horizontal force H at the pivot; and so forth. Apart from these variable quantities, certain constants are also involved: the length of the pole (L), and the masses of the pole (m) and the vehicle (M).

The mathematical model then consists of a system of four nonlinear differential equations. As an example, one of them is

$$H = my'' + m(L/2)(\theta'' \cos \theta - \theta'^2 \sin \theta).$$

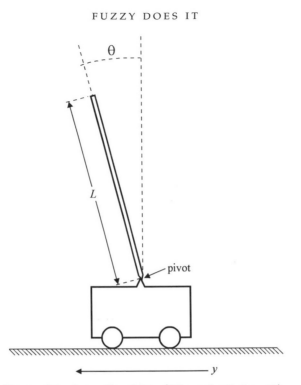

FIGURE I.6. A small vehicle ("the robot's hand") with a rigid pole ("the stick") joined to it by a pivot. It can move back and forth along a rectilinear track.

The correct velocity, that is, how fast and in which direction the vehicle must move to balance the pole, results from solving these equations. Practical methods to solve the system of equations using a digital computer are available. But to prevent the pole from falling, especially a short and light one, the answer must be calculated almost instantly. In other words, the equations need to be solved in real time, a feat beyond the power of present-day computers. So much for exact mathematical models. Enter fuzzy logic.

Instead of using differential equations, Yamakawa based his approach on a linguistic model of the system. This model has two input variables: the angle θ and its derivative θ' (in simple terms, θ' measures how fast the pole is falling or rising). The output or control variable is the velocity of the vehicle (y').

25

The values of these variables are signed numbers, that is, they can be positive, negative, or zero. The sign of θ, for example, tells in which direction the pole is tilted: forward $(+)$, backward $(-)$, or neither (0), that is, it is vertical; the sign of y' indicates whether the vehicle should move forward $(+)$, backward $(-)$, or stand still (0); and the sign of θ' depends on which sense (i.e., clockwise or counterclockwise) the pole is rotating.

As a first step in constructing the linguistic model, the actions taken instinctively by a human to balance the pole are analyzed and expressed in the form of operating rules. In effect, we tell the robot how to move its hand depending on the "error" (i.e., the angle θ with the vertical) and on its rate of change (θ'). The beauty of it is that we can put the instructions in everyday language. For example:

$$\text{"If the pole is balanced, do not move your hand."} \qquad (7)$$

Next, the intuitive relationships among the variables are encoded in terms of fuzzy sets. These are labeled negative large (NL), negative medium (NM), negative small (NS), zero (ZR), positive small (PS), positive medium (PM), and positive large (PL). Thus, (7) becomes the fuzzy inference rule:

$$\text{If } \theta \text{ is } ZR \text{ and } \theta' \text{ is } ZR \text{ then } y' \text{ is } ZR. \qquad (8)$$

(A balanced pole is vertical $(\theta = 0)$ and it is not moving $(\theta' = 0)$; since the "hand" should not move, its velocity (y') must be zero.)

Another rule of thumb is: "If the pole is slightly tilted away from you and falling slowly, move your hand forward but not too quickly," which is translated as:

$$\text{If } \theta \text{ is } PS \text{ and } \theta' \text{ is } PS \text{ then } y' \text{ is } PS. \qquad (9)$$

Besides (8) and (9), Yamakawa's linguistic model of the control actions comprises five other rules; all of them are listed in table 1.

Unlike the mathematical model previously discussed, the linguistic model does not explicitly involve any equations or numerical values. Another difference between the two models concerns their a priori performance. While we can demonstrate theoretically that the solution of the differential equations does balance the pole, no such proof seems possible regarding the linguistic model. In other words, no one can tell in advance whether or not the fuzzy inference algorithm

TABLE 1

Seven linguistic rules to balance an inverted pendulum.
For example, Rule 4: If the angle is positive small and
the angular velocity is negative small, then the
velocity of the vehicle is zero.

Rule No.	Angle (θ)	Angular Velocity (θ')	Velocity of Vehicle (y')
1	ZR	ZR	ZR
2	PS	PS	PS
3	PM	ZR	PM
4	PS	NS	ZR
5	NM	ZR	NM
6	NS	NS	NS
7	NS	PS	ZR

Notes:
 NS = negative small
 NM = negative medium
 PS = positive small
 PM = positive medium
 ZR = zero

based on the seven linguistic rules of table 1—or some other similar set of rules—will achieve its goal of balancing the pole. Success—or failure—is only established experimentally: run the system and see what happens.

If a given set of inference rules fails to do the job, try a new set (it is easier to produce control rules than to solve nonlinear differential equations). Notice that if we were to tell the robot what to do for each possible input condition, we would end up with 49 rules (since each one of θ, θ' can take on seven linguistic values). It is one of the realities of the fuzzy method that a relatively small number of rules usually suffices to achieve control. An alternative to this trial-and-error approach is the automatic search for an optimal set of rules. The most popular such techniques are based on neural networks and genetic algorithms (the subject of part 3).

But identifying a correct set of control rules is not enough. If effective control is to be accomplished, the performance of the fuzzy inference algorithm must be extremely fast. In order to achieve almost instantaneous execution, Yamakawa designed the world's first high-speed fuzzy controller. By rotating switches, the controller can be programmed to execute any desired set of up to fifteen rules involving the seven fuzzy labels from *NS* (negative small) to *PL* (positive large). The membership function of each fuzzy set is implemented by a circuit. The output signal of this circuit, ranging from 0 to 5 volts, corresponds to the membership grades from 0.0 to 1.0. Fifteen "rule" chips perform the fuzzy inferences and one "defuzzifier" chip converts their conclusions into an analogue numerical value (the fuzzy inference algorithm and defuzzification are explained in the next section). Thanks to its parallel architecture, the controller can respond to a change in input in less than a microsecond. This corresponds to a "deduction" speed of a million fuzzy decisions per second.

To demonstrate the efficiency of his controller, Yamakawa applied it to the stabilization of the pole, the so-called inverted pendulum control problem. Here is how his balancing-act system operates. A sensor measures the angle θ of the pole with the vertical, calculates its derivative θ', and feeds this information to the controller. From this data, the rule chips perform the seven fuzzy inferences specified in table 1 and the defuzzifier chip calculates the (nonfuzzy) output. This numerical value determines the rotating speed of the servo motor that moves the small vehicle back and forth.

The high-speed fuzzy controller successfully balanced short and long pendulums. The short one was 5 millimeters in diameter, 15 centimeters in length, and had a weight of 3.5 grams; the other was twice as thick, 50 cm in length, and weighed 50 grams. The same set of control rules worked in both cases, even though the poles had different length and weight. This suggests the suitability of fuzzy control to handle systems with time-variant parameters such as trains or tanks, which can be more or less full. Moreover, the controller proved it can tolerate some hardware malfunction or defect as well as slight programming mistakes. For even after deleting one of the rules or making a minor change in a fuzzy value (from positive large to positive medium, say), the system performed well, although it was less stable.

Yamakawa's fuzzy logic controller and pole-balancing system was manufactured by the electronics company Omron for demonstration at the Second World Congress of the International Fuzzy Systems Association (IFSA). The meeting, which took place in Tokyo in the summer of 1987, served as a showcase for the practical applications of fuzzy logic. It also foreshadowed the "fuzzy boom" of consumer goods of the late 1980s and early 1990s, by making Japanese industry aware of the commercial potential of the new technique. From video cameras to air conditioners and washing machines, "fuzzy" products, featuring technology based on fuzzy logic, will soon inundate the Japanese market.

The Magic of Fuzzy Inference

> If we only seek to gain power over things, we can resign
> ourselves to incomprehension, for we can act effectively
> without understanding the reasons of our success.
> *(René Thom)*[8]

The crucial step in the implementation of a fuzzy inference rule is to give it a mathematical form. This is usually done by interpreting

if x is A and y is B then z is C

as describing a procedure that generates a new fuzzy subset C' (the "conclusion") from given fuzzy subsets A' and B' (the data). The procedure is often presented in the form of a phony logical deduction or "fuzzy" inference:

Rule: if x is A and y is B then z is C
Premises: x is A', y is B'
Conclusion: z is C'.

In most applications, the values of x and y are numbers x_0 and y_0 resulting from measuring speed, angle, voltage, or some other (numerical) variable. Then, the premises "x is A'" and "y is B'" become "x is (equal to) x_0" and "y is (equal to) y_0," and the membership function of the fuzzy subset C' is defined by the equation

$$C'(z) = \min\{ A(x_0), B(y_0), C(z)\}. \tag{10}$$

That is, the grade of membership in C' of the number z is the smallest, or minimum, of the grades $A(x_0), B(y_0), C(z)$.

Applications of fuzzy logic to real-life problems generally require more than one inference rule—Mamdani used fifteen linguistic rules to control the operation of his steam engine. For given input values x_0 and y_0, each rule will yield a fuzzy subset (calculated as in (10) above) which may be seen as the contribution of that particular rule to the final decision. These fuzzy subsets, or partial conclusions, are then combined into a single final conclusion D using the fuzzy union operation (see Operations on Fuzzy Sets):

$$D = C_1' \cup C_2' \cup \cdots C_n', \tag{11}$$

where C_1' is the conclusion of rule 1, C_2' is the conclusion of rule 2, and so on. Since the control action generally consists in the appropriate setting of pressure, temperature, charge, etc., the value of the output variable z must be a single number z_0 ("fuzzy" control is really exact control calculated from fuzzy rules). The number z_0 is computed from the above fuzzy set D by a "defuzzification" procedure. One of the most widely used is the so-called center of gravity method: If the fuzzy subset D is represented by its membership function (see figure I.7), its center of gravity is the number z_0 such that the vertical line through z_0 divides the graph into two regions of equal area.

The above scheme for calculating an output value z_0 from input values x_0 and y_0 is called the fuzzy inference algorithm. To illustrate

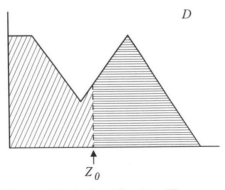

FIGURE I.7. Defuzzification. The vertical line through the point z_0 (the center of gravity) divides the graph of D into two regions of equal area.

it in a very simple case (for a more detailed analysis, see Appendix 1), we consider a fictitious system with input variables x and y, output variable z, and two fuzzy sets: "approximately zero" and "small positive" whose membership functions appear in figure I.8. The relationships between the three variables are described by two linguistic rules:

Rule 1: If x is approximately zero and y is small positive, then z is approximately zero;

Rule 2: If x is small positive and y is approximately zero, then z is small positive.

What is the optimal value of z if $x = 0.8$ and $y = 0.4$ (as measured by some sensors, say)? The conclusion of the fuzzy inference is the fuzzy set D on the far right of the figure, and its center of gravity is the number 0.7. The fuzzy inference algorithm has therefore allowed us to "deduce" that if x is 0.8 and y is 0.4, then z should be 0.7.

(If at this point the reader is trying to understand why this algorithm manages to effectively control certain real systems, then he or she has plenty of company: A well-kept secret is that practically no one really understands why the algorithm works.)

A fuzzy control algorithm is generally highly "robust." This means that it can tolerate certain changes (in the operations, the membership functions, or system parameters) without significantly affecting the overall performance of the controller.

Many other algorithms that incorporate fuzzy set theoretic ideas and techniques have worked well in practice. For instance, the fuzzy algorithm that controls the speed of the automatic trains[9] in the Japanese city of Sendai employs twelve rules of the type

$$\text{if } (u = c \text{ implies } x \text{ is } A \text{ and } y \text{ is } B) \text{ then } u = c$$

where A and B are fuzzy sets that evaluate the performance of the system and c is a nonfuzzy control command. From the input data (time, position, velocity, etc.) the algorithm assigns to each rule a number between 0 and 1—the rule's "likelihood." Then, the control command c of the most likely rule is executed (for example, the

31

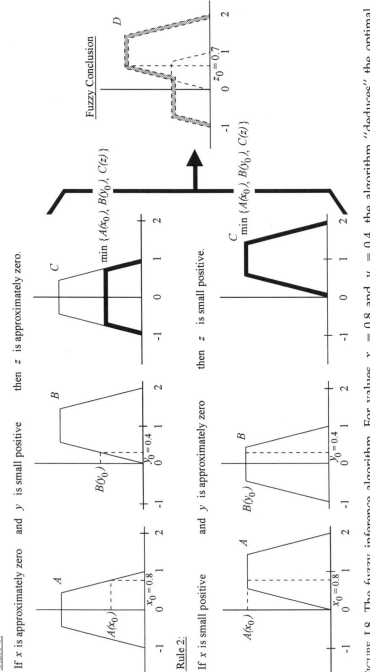

FIGURE I.8. The fuzzy inference algorithm. For values $x_0 = 0.8$ and $y_0 = 0.4$, the algorithm "deduces" the optimal value 0.7 of z from the two given fuzzy rules.

brake is set at notch no. 9). The program that implements the algorithm on a microcomputer calculates a control command every 100 milliseconds.

FUZZY LOGIC GOES COMMERCIAL

By the end of 1990, the number of practical applications of fuzzy logic in Japan was estimated at between two and three hundred. An important number of these were consumer goods, which at the same time contributed to make "fuzzy" a household word in Japan. "The fuzzy age has begun!" proclaimed a commercial for the Aisaigo Day Fuzzy washing machine, manufactured by Matsushita. It is interesting to note that commercial ads used the English word "fuzzy," instead of the Japanese equivalent "aimai." This proved to be a successful marketing ploy and soon any product that called itself fuzzy was a hit.

But the notion of a fuzzy product is itself fuzzy. For the most part, these are electronic devices that incorporate some degree of fuzzy control—although it is not always clear how much: 10 percent, 50 percent, or 1 percent? Their main features are simplicity of operation and "smart" behavior. The user has only to turn on the machine, after which it will literally control itself and respond with human common sense to changing conditions, in most cases outperforming conventional models.

When it is time to do the laundry, for instance, you can trust the fuzzy chip to decide the best way to do it. Just load the National washing machine and push the button. An optical sensor will detect the type and the degree of dirt from the muddiness of the water. Other sensors will ascertain the size of the load and the kind of detergent being used. On this information, the fuzzy inference rules will select the water level and other settings for the best and most economical cycle. The manufacturer promises a perfect wash with substantial savings on electricity. (Unfortunately, the machine will not warn you if you happen to mix items that should not be washed together, in which case be prepared for some fuzzy colors at the end of the wash ...)

The automatic iris of a Sanyo camcorder responds more effectively to complex lighting conditions by exploiting the flexibility of fuzzy sets. In conventional systems there are only two degrees of "brightness": 0, if the illuminance is less than 1000 lux, and 1 if it equals or exceeds 1000. Thus, illuminance levels that are close to each other, but on different sides of the dividing line, result in degrees of brightness which are far apart. With a fuzzy membership function the degrees increase smoothly from 0 to 1, so such jumps do not occur. Overall brightness is evaluated using rules that determine the priority of different areas of the image under various conditions. These inference rules involve fuzzy concepts such as "small" brightness or two degrees of brightness being "close" to each other. The camera can therefore compensate for backlight or excess frontlight better than those based on all-or-nothing brightness estimation.

In September 1989, Toshiba Corporation announced a scheduling system for elevators based on a fuzzy controller supported by a conventional expert system. Designed to manage up to eight cars, the Command-AI system promised to reduce waiting time in a high-rise building by optimally assigning an elevator in response to each call. "With this new fuzzy system," the information brochure claimed, "the possibility of having to wait more than 60 seconds is reduced by 30 percent [compared to their standard system]."

The photocopying process that most users take for granted (how did they ever manage in the Dark Ages before photocopying machines?) is a delicate one. The electrical and optical processes taking place are influenced, among other factors, by the temperature, the condition of the toner, and the image density (the black/white ratio) of the document to be copied. If these variables are not properly controlled, the copy may be of inferior or even very poor quality. In conventional machines, the necessary adjustments must be done manually by a qualified technician. In a model released by Canon in October 1990, a fuzzy logic system performs the appropriate settings, to insure that the transfer of the toner to the photocopying paper by static electricity is done under optimal conditions. A sensor measures the temperature while a potentiometer picks up the image density of the document. Nine fuzzy inference rules are then used to "deduce" the right charge (potential) of the photoconductor drum. For instance, "if temperature is low and image density is high, then charge is medium." The manufacturer claimed that the resulting system not only eliminated the need for manual adjustment but that it also reduced the number of paper jams, while maintaining a uniform copy quality.

The fuzzy frenzy covered the whole spectrum of consumer goods, including television sets that adjust volume according to noise level and viewer's distance, fuzzy microwave ovens and vacuum cleaners; and video cameras capable of bringing the subject into focus no matter where it appears in the picture frame (the wonders of fuzzy focusing).

Many other practical uses of fuzzy logic were being tested during that period, from helping the motion of a robot[10] to controlling the tracking of a VCR.[11] A number of these were prototypes and it is hard to tell whether they ever got past the experimental stage. At any rate, by one expert's estimate[12] the number of fuzzy products marketed in Japan during the period 1989–93 exceeded six hundred. This claim brings us back to the tricky question of evaluating the fuzzy component of a self-proclaimed "fuzzy" product, and to the most basic one of what constitutes an "application" of a given theory. If digital computers are used to schedule oil production, should we count this as an industrial application of binary arithmetic and Boolean algebra or as an application of transistors and electronic circuits?

For all the wonders of the theory of fuzzy sets, most so-called applications of fuzzy logic would simply not exist without the advanced technology of sensors, chips, and high-speed computing. But whatever the merit of the theory in making so many smart and easy-to-use products a reality, Japanese engineers are rightly proud of having set new standards of design and performance. "As far as fuzzy is concerned," says Masato Nakayashiki, managing director of the Laboratory for International Fuzzy Engineering Research (LIFE) in Yokohama, "no one can claim that Japan is imitating foreign technology."

Like all booms that deserve the name, the fuzzy boom eventually subsided, at least as far as media attention was concerned. Given the extensive coverage that the new technology had received, in Japan and elsewhere, it was predictable that "fuzzy" would no longer be news by the end of 1991.

Nakayashiki reflects on the social dimension of the phenomenon: "The fuzzy boom was supported by highly emotional elements. These may have included excessive expectations or bona fide misunderstandings that view fuzzy technology as magic. Nevertheless, in this reaction one detects people's desire for simplicity, friendliness and humanity in technology."[13]

35

From the larger perspective of all human beings—and not just well-off consumers—improving the performance of home appliances, elevators, and automobiles which were already among the world's most advanced appears as a rather frivolous application of the theory. Nonetheless, it was through these down-to-earth uses that ordinary people became aware of the existence and practical implications of a mathematical idea: the notion of a fuzzy set.

Fuzzy Inputs

The inputs x_0 and y_0 to the fuzzy inference algorithm are typically numbers that measure certain scalar quantities, such as temperature or voltage. In control applications, these numbers are obtained without direct human intervention using sensors or other automatic devices. The first stage of the algorithm then "fuzzifies" the crisp data x_0 and y_0 by calculating their membership grades in various fuzzy sets. There are cases, however, in which the input data are already fuzzy. This situation occurs, for example, when a human expert must estimate to what degree, from 0 to 1, a certain characteristic or feature is present, as in the following application of fuzzy inference to medical diagnosis.

For the initial screening of prostatic cancer, doctors may use both a rectal examination and the images obtained by ultrasonic techniques. But the clinical assessment of ultrasonic images, even if done by a qualified physician, remains highly subjective. To allow for a more objective appraisal, a team of Japanese doctors developed a diagnostic system based on fuzzy logic which can be implemented on a personal computer.[14]

A rectal probe with a scanner is used to transmit transverse images of the prostate. The physician then estimates certain features of the image, for example whether the shape is smooth (membership grade $g = 0$), disrupted ($g = 1$), or somewhere in between ($0 < g < 1$). The appraised fuzzy value is entered by moving a pointer along the computer image of a line segment representing the interval [0, 1], and clicking at the appropriate point. Based on the general rules for ultrasonic diagnosis used by expert urologists, the algorithm calculates a numerical output. Depending on this number, the patient is declared healthy, suffering from prostatic cancer, or a "fuzzy case," that is, too close to call, if the test was inconclusive.

Clinical trials of the system are reportedly very encouraging. For example, the computer verdict resulted in only one false negative case and two cases in the fuzzy zone, when tried on thirty patients with confirmed prostatic cancer. The quantification of vagueness and subjectivity, which lie at the heart of the fuzzy approach, proved once again an efficient way of automating the making of a decision.

Opinion polls is another field which could benefit from the flexibility of fuzzy inputs. When people are consulted about a particular issue—the death penalty, say—they are usually asked to choose among a small number of answers: strongly in favor, somewhat in favor, strongly opposed, and so forth. In the extreme case of referendums there are only two possible choices, yes or no. It is either all or nothing, black or white, while in reality many people stand somewhere in between the two extremes.

By permitting the answer to be a number between 0 (= No) and 1 (= Yes), undecided voters could express their uncertainty and hesitations ("yes but," "rather not," etc.). Such split votes would be counted as giving a fraction of support to each of the options, such as 0.75 Yes/0.25 No. By way of example of what might happen, suppose that the outcome of a conventional referendum was 54 percent to 46 percent in favor of Yes. If one-third of those who voted Yes could have given a less categorical answer, say 0.75 Yes/0.25 No (instead of 1 Yes/0 No), then the outcome would have been reversed, with the No side winning by 50.5 to 49.5 percent. Many other distributions of the uncertainty are of course possible. By quantifying the degree of conviction of each ballot, the will of the people should be better gauged and democracy better served.[15]

Profit also might be better served by allowing people to express gradations of preferences. Consumer's Edge, a California software developer, hopes to offer "deep interviews" on the Internet—extensive questions-and-answers to match consumers to products. If you are in the market for, say, an automobile, the program informs you that there are 746 possible cars. Then it starts asking how much you want to spend, how important is air conditioning, power steering, anti-lock brakes, and so forth. The answers are not just yes or no; you can express partial preference by sliding a dial to the left or right with your mouse.[16]

37

FUZZY ENGINEERING COMES TO LIFE

*As science and technology progress, we expect to be able to
instill into machines some of the good human qualities.
Besides being smart, we would like them to be friendly,
thoughtful, tolerant, perhaps even to show sympathy and
understanding. But what if, as machines become more like us
in some respects, it turns out to be impossible to filter out the
darker side of human nature: selfishness, intolerance,
wickedness—the list is long.*

At the beginning of 1989, as the industrial and commercial applications of fuzzy logic were spreading, the Japanese government persuaded a vast consortium of international companies to create a new
center for research and development on fuzzy computing. And so the
Laboratory for International Fuzzy Engineering Research (LIFE) was
established in March 1989 as a private corporation with special tax
exemptions. Its forty-nine industrial members included most major
Japanese companies (Matsushita, Canon, Hitachi, Mitsubishi, etc.).

The early successes of fuzzy methods were seen as a prelude to
even more dramatic achievements. The new center would coordinate
the efforts of government, industry, and academic institutions to
realize those expectations—and cash in on the results. Located in the
port city of Yokohama, on the west side of Tokyo Bay, LIFE was to
develop applications of fuzzy theory to engineering, from basic research to experimental production and evaluation. The laboratory
sought to promote interest in fuzzy methods through technological
exchange with Japanese and foreign companies. To fulfill its mission,
it was given six years and a $50-million budget.

Toshiro Terano, who was the director of research during LIFE's life
span, calls "fuzzy engineering" the combination of fuzzy logic, used
as a tool, and systems engineering, a methodology for dealing glob-
ally with complex problems. Fuzzy engineering favors a qualitative
representation of the main aspects of a problem, followed by a
"fuzzy" solution strategy, similar to human reasoning, which can
subsequently be coded as an algorithm or in some other mathematical form. "The necessity of fuzzy engineering," Terano says, "depends on how much the human factor is taken into account by the
engineer designing a system."

This preoccupation with the human element persisted throughout LIFE's existence and might have been intended by the choice of the acronym—attributed to Michio Sugeno, a professor at the Tokyo Institute of Technology, who must also be credited with the idea of creating the laboratory. Indeed, LIFE's primary concern has been to place the human being at the center of an information-oriented society. Its main research projects aimed at developing systems that support a person's decisions or actions through two-way communication in everyday language between human and machine. This perspective raises the problem of processing the ambiguity inherent in natural language, the questions of meaning and subjectivity, and even the role of emotions. One of LIFE's postulates was the belief that fuzzy methods hold the key to the design of intelligent machines, artificial brains whose capabilities would be similar in some respects to those of the human mind. While other approaches to machine intelligence seek to model the physiological aspects of the brain, fuzzy engineering focuses on its psychological function.

SPECULATING ON FUZZY DECISIONS

LIFE initially concentrated its research efforts in three areas: decision support systems (which included fuzzy control), the development of intelligent robots, and the design of a fuzzy computer which could execute fuzzy operations (such as fuzzy set operations or fuzzy arithmetic) at high speed. Research was oriented toward solving concrete problems, rather than elaborating abstract theories.

Among the specific projects in the first area, LIFE's researchers developed a decision system for foreign exchange trading. The forecasting of exchange rates is typical of a real-world complex problem not amenable to mathematical modeling. Apart from numerical data (interest rates, trade balances, etc.), fluctuations in rates are also influenced by non-numerical information. The latter includes remarks made by financial authorities, real or apprehended political decisions, and international news. Psychological factors, such as the exchange dealer's perception of the market, must be taken into account as well.

The resulting fuzzy expert system incorporated the complex relationships of some three hundred variables expressed in the form of fuzzy inference rules. For instance: "If the U.S. Federal Reserve Bank rates are high and the official discount rate is low, then American short-term interest rates become very high." The expertise of foreign exchange dealers and other market officials, mathematical models of economic theories, and the analysis of case studies all intervened in the formulation of the five thousand fuzzy rules. Trial runs of the system gave satisfactory results—if one excludes computation time as a performance factor.[17] But even if the technology developed is not yet ready to be used in actual situations, people at LIFE believe that no other approach would have produced a system with comparable performance.

THE FUZZY CHOPPER

During its second period of existence, from 1992 to 1995, the laboratory's research projects focused on the general theme of developing human-friendly information systems. Efforts were split on two somewhat overlapping fronts: making smart machines and enhancing the communication between human and computer.

One of the intelligent robots developed jointly at LIFE and at the Tokyo Institute of Technology took the form of a small helicopter that can execute verbal commands given in natural language, like "hover" or "fly forward a short distance." The ultimate goal of this long-term project is to develop an automatic flight controller which would be able to handle qualitative as well as quantitative information. Guided by such a device, the helicopter would possess a large degree of autonomy, allowing it to perform critical tasks in bad weather and other environmental conditions too dangerous for a human pilot. And since the robot would "understand" natural language, it could be directed by someone with little experience—a definite advantage over standard radio-controlled models, whose successful operation requires months of training.

A helicopter is intrinsically an unstable system—not just up in the air, for its own vibrations can be fed back to it when it is on the ground. In order to stabilize it and steer it, the pilot must adjust both the speed and the pitch of the rotor blades according to the desired flight mode (hover, forward, leftward, etc.). This is achieved through the skillful use of sticks, pedals, and levers. Helicopter flying dynamics is extremely difficult to describe analytically due to the strong

40

interrelation (or, *cross-coupling*, in technical jargon) of the various flight modes—for example, flying forward may affect the lateral stability. The fuzzy approach, which bypasses an explicit mathematical description of the system's dynamics, becomes then a natural choice for the control strategy. After all, a human pilot succeeds without any mathematical model of the process.

The linguistic rules that form the knowledge base of the fuzzy controller were first formulated with the help of operation manuals and interviews with experienced pilots. "If the body rolls right, then move the lateral stick leftward" and "If the body pitches forward, then move the longitudinal stick backwards" are typical rules for hovering. These rules were then tested and refined using a helicopter flight simulator, and the numerical parameters adjusted as a result of actual field experiments. The whole design process was also guided by a knowledge of the physical laws governing the motion of rigid bodies.

A set of onboard sensors measure angles, velocities, accelerations, and other relevant variables. Based on these data, the fuzzy controller performs the actions of a human pilot in response to voice commands. "The" controller is in fact a combination of several fuzzy controllers organized in a hierarchical fashion. For example, one of these controllers governs yawing, or the angle off the right course, which a human pilot can adjust by depressing a pedal. During automatic operation, the input data are the error—the difference between the sensor reading and the correct angle—and the rate of change of this error. The pedal is then regulated by the fuzzy controller depending on the output of a fuzzy inference involving nine linguistic rules. "If error is zero and rate of change is positive then pedal is negative medium" is one of them. Other sets of rules control altitude, rolling angle, velocity, and so forth. A fuzzy flight manager integrates the outputs of the various fuzzy inferences and helps to smooth the transitions between flight modes.

The small helicopter—3.5 meters long and with a payload of only 20 kilograms—is still in the experimental stages. Several flight modes (hover, forward, circle, and stop) have already been tested, while additional modes, such as takeoff and landing, have yet to be implemented. But in the end, the true significance of projects like this does not necessarily lie in their practical realization. They rather serve as prototypes of complex systems on which to explore the possibilities

—and the limits—of fuzzy techniques. As the authors themselves put it in the conclusion of one of their progress reports: "What we have learned thus far is that a fuzzy hierarchical controller design can successfully control a highly coupled system with only qualitative information of the plant and without an explicit mathematical expression of the model."[18]

AfterLIFE

In early 1995, as originally planned, LIFE ceased to exist. Its most important legacy may be to have demonstrated the potential of the fuzzy approach in the development of systems with a high level of intelligence. Building on the methods and ideas developed during the laboratory's six short years of existence, many challenging conceptions might become a reality in the not-so-distant future. Smart wheelchairs, voice navigation systems to guide the blind, and other intelligent devices for the handicapped; the generation of images using natural language to assist the creative process in design, computer graphics, and virtual reality; software that can automatically summarize the contents of news stories, articles, and reports by extracting certain features, and robots that are able to act on simple instructions by inferring the human's intentions are just a few of the projects envisaged by LIFE's researchers.[19]

Toshiro Terano's twenty years' experience with the success of fuzzy methods in solving concrete problems have convinced him of their usefulness. But he admits that they still lack widespread recognition. "The attempts, in fuzzy engineering, to introduce and actively utilize fuzziness in a system have never been accepted by mainstream science," he says. No matter. His faith in the power of fuzzy techniques remains as strong as ever. In the future, he expects computers to assist humans by providing information that is not just correct but also meaningful; information that will stimulate the mind and increase knowledge and creativity. This will be accomplished through a user-machine dialogue in everyday language similar to the one that occurs naturally between humans. And LIFE's former Director of Research believes that fuzzy engineering has a unique contribution to make toward the achievement of such an ambitious goal. LIFE is dead, long live fuzzy engineering!

A Personal Perspective

In the spring of 1996, addressing a meeting of experts at the Berkeley campus of the University of California, Lotfi Zadeh reflected on the evolution of fuzzy logic from his privileged personal perspective. As early as 1962, three years before the publication of his seminal paper on fuzzy sets, he had called attention to the need for a radically different kind of mathematics: "the mathematics of fuzzy or cloudy quantities." This new mathematics would be used to study what he called animate systems, especially situations involving human language, decisions, and reasoning. Some thirty years later, he was pleased with the progress made but recognized that "we are merely scratching the surface." And he added, "By restricting ourselves to classical techniques we simply cannot bridge the gap. We can do more today thanks to fuzzy logic, neural networks, genetic algorithms and so forth, but we need to do much more."

Zadeh offered a practical example of a problem that might be impossible to solve with classical techniques alone: the fraudulent call problem. An unauthorized person places a telephone call using the password of a customer C, who is then billed for the call. Given a record of C's telephone calls, how can the telephone company detect that the call was "abnormal"? By observing that "abnormality" is a fuzzy concept, Zadeh predicted that only a neuro-fuzzy system might be able to solve this problem.

There is much experimentation going on with various kinds of "hybrid" systems, which combine the advantages of two or more soft techniques. The marriage of fuzzy logic and neural networks, or neuro-fuzzy, is one of the most popular unions. For example, neural networks can be used to "learn" the fuzzy membership functions that result in the best performance of the system. But we are jumping the gun here. Neural networks will be properly introduced in part 3. For now, we shall take a look at the limits of digital computers.

Notes

1. J. P. Aurrand-Lions, L. Fournier, P. Jarri, M. de Saint Blancard, and E. Sanchez, "Application of Fuzzy Control for ISIS Vehicle Braking,"

Proceedings of the Fourth World Congress of the International Fuzzy Systems Association IFSA '91, Engineering Volume, pp. 9–12, R. Lowen and M. Roubens, eds., Brussels, 1991.

2. Andreas Bastian, "Fuzzy Logic in Automatic Transmission Control," *Vehicle Systems Dynamics* 24 (1995), pp. 389–400.

3. E. H. Mamdani and S. Assilian, "An Experiment in Linguistic Synthesis with a Fuzzy Logic Controller," *Int. J. Man-Machine Studies* (1975), 7, 1–13.

4. D. A. Watermann, "Generalisation Learning Techniques for Automating the Learning of Heuristics," *Artificial Intelligence*, vol. 1 (1970), pp. 121–70.

5. E. H. Mamdani, "Process Control Using Fuzzy Logic," in *Fuzzy Sets: Theory and Applications to Policy Analysis and Information Systems*, Paul P. Wang and S. K. Chang, eds., Plenum Press, New York and London (1980), pp. 240–65.

6. S. Yasunobu, S. Miyamoto, and H. Ihara, "Fuzzy Control for Automatic Train Operation System," IFAC Control in Transportation Systems, pp. 33–39, Baden-Baden, Federal Republic of Germany, 1983.

7. Takeshi Yamakawa, "Stabilization of an inverted pendulum by a high-speed fuzzy logic controller hardware system," *Fuzzy Sets and Systems* 32 (1989), 161–80.

8. René Thom, "La magie contemporaine," in *La magie contemporaine—l'échec du savoir moderne*, Y. Johannisse, ed., Québec/Amérique, 1994.

9. S. Yasunobu and S. Miyamoto, "Automatic Train Operation by Predictive Fuzzy Control." In M. Sugeno, ed., *Industrial Applications of Fuzzy Control*, pp. 1–18. North-Holland, Amsterdam, 1985.

10. R. Tanscheit and E. M. Scharf, "Experiments with the Use of a Rule-Based Self-Organising Controller for Robotics Applications," *Fuzzy Sets and Systems* 26 (1988), 195–214.

11. Tadafusa Tomitaka, "Tracking Control for VCRs," *Proceedings of the Fourth World Congress of the International Fuzzy Systems Association IFSA '91*, Engineering Volume, pp. 227–30, R. Lowen and M. Roubens, eds., Brussels, 1991.

12. Masato Nakayashiki, "On Fuzzy," *LIFE Technical News*, November 1993, vol. 4, no. 1, Laboratory for International Fuzzy Engineering Research, Yokohama, Japan, p. 13.

13. Ibid.

14. Tomoaki Fujioka, Seizaburo Arita, Taiichi Saito et al., "Transrectal Ultrasonography of Prostatic Cancer: Application of a New Diagnostic Item and Fuzzy Inference," *Jpn. J. Med. Ultrasonics* 17(suppl.), 1990, 165–66.

15. Arturo Sangalli, "Vote, Vote, Vote for Fuzzy Logic," *New Scientist*, vol. 144, no. 1951, November 12, 1994.

16. "The Web's Middleman," *Time* magazine, February 17, 1997, p. 51.

17. A. Ralescu, ed., *Applied Research in Fuzzy Technology*, Kluwer Academic Publishers, 1994.

18. M. Sugeno, M. F. Griffin, and A. Bastian, "Fuzzy Hierarchical Control of An Unmanned Helicopter," *Proceedings of the Fifth World Congress of the International Fuzzy Systems Association (IFSA)*, pp. 179–82, Seoul, South Korea, 1993.

19. Toshiro Terano, "Fuzzy Engineering—Its Progress at LIFE and Future Prospects," IEEE/IFES '95 Conference, Yokohama, Japan, March 1995.

PART TWO
LIMITS

*

CHAPTER THREE

The Limits of Classical Computing

AN OLD DREAM BECOMES A REALITY

IN 1936, the British mathematician Alan Turing and the American logician Alonzo Church came up, independently and almost simultaneously, with mathematical definitions of what is meant by a numerical function to be "computable." Although different in form, both definitions turned out to have the same meaning, suggesting that they had managed to capture some fundamental concept whose time had come. Turing's and Church's breakthrough opened the way to a rigorous study of computability, a theory that is still very much alive today.

The idea of building a machine to execute arithmetic operations occurred to many scientists, engineers, and philosophers at various places and times in human history. One of the first to put this idea into practice appears to have been the German astronomer Wilhem Schickard. A contemporary of Kepler, Schickard built in 1623 what he called a Computing Clock, capable of performing addition, subtraction, multiplication, and division by entirely mechanical means. But Schickard's invention had a short life: a fire destroyed it barely one year later. In his *Histoire universelle des chiffres*, Georges Ifrah[1] speculates that the fire might not have been an unfortunate accident but the deliberate work of a human hand in a futile attempt to prevent a machine from calculating—a faculty that was seen by the forces of obscurantism as the exclusive prerogative of the human mind. Shortly afterward, in 1642, the French mathematician and philosopher Blaise Pascal, then only nineteen, constructed an adding machine made up of a series of gears—the Pascaline—to help with his father's bookkeeping. The main purpose of these and similar automata was to liberate the astronomer, the bookkeeper, or the engineer from the tedious (and error-prone) task of carrying out by hand lengthy numerical manipulations. In time, these machines would also permit ordinary people to practice the art of arithmetic without having to learn complicated rules of operation with numbers.

Many other attempts at realizing the dream of mechanical calculation followed, but the title of father of artificial computing is generally reserved for the English mathematician Charles Babbage, who
early in the nineteenth century conceived the theoretical and practical
principles of an automatic computing device—a true forerunner of
present-day computers. He then spent the remaining fifty years of his
life trying without success to actually construct one.

If Babbage's ingenious creations were never viable, some blame it
on the technical limitations of Victorian mechanical engineering,
especially on the lack of machinery precise enough to manufacture
the components at the heart of his elaborate "engines"—as he called
them. Babbage's Difference Engine, for instance, would have weighed
several tons when completed, and its estimated twenty-five thousand
parts, once assembled into a precise system of gears, racks, cams, and
levers, would have stood eight feet high, seven feet long, and three
feet deep. The original purpose of the machine, a precursor of his
more advanced Analytical Engine, was to compute navigational and
other arithmetical tables. These were in growing demand from engineers, bankers, and merchants in the rapidly developing worlds of
commerce and industry. In fact, Babbage's initial motivation for
automating the calculations was not so much to improve the efficiency of the process as to guarantee its accuracy. His machine was
supposed to supply a mold in which stereotype plates of the computed tables could be cast, in order to prevent the printing errors so
frequent in manually typeset tables. Less than twenty years after the
French Revolution, the idea of automatic typesetting had already
been born.

Over the course of time, from one unfinished prototype to another,
Babbage incorporated in his creations the major ideas upon which all
modern digital computers are constructed, notably the five basic
units of a computer: the store, containing the data, instructions, and
intermediate calculations; the processor (or mill), "into which," in
Babbage's own words, "the quantities to be operated upon are
always brought"; a unit which controls the whole operation (by
means of a Jacquard loom system); the input (by means of punched
cards); and the output, which automatically prints results. These
fundamental principles were subsequently forgotten, only to be redis-
covered in the middle of the twentieth century. In January 1943, more
than one hundred years after Babbage first dreamed of an automatic,

multipurpose computing device, a real machine featuring those characteristics was finally a reality. Conceived by Howard Aiken, a professor of physics at Harvard University, and built with the help of IBM engineers, the Harvard Mark I worked on principles inspired by those of Babbage's Analytical Engine.

"Charles Babbage always sought to provide a mathematical approach to each of the many and varied problems which he tackled," writes J. M. Dubbey in *The Mathematical Works of Charles Babbage*. And he adds, "Whether discussing miracles, pin-making, postal services, geology, economics, politics or even his private life, he always attempted to formulate a problem in as mathematical a way as possible."

A man of vision as well as a practical genius, Babbage prophetically predicted the tremendous success of computing machines—someone else's, if not his own. "If I survive some few years longer," he wrote seven years before his death in 1871, "the Analytical Engine will exist, and its works will afterwards be spread over the world."

CAN MACHINES COMPUTE EVERYTHING?

Computers can do some amazing things, but from a mathematical point of view we are only interested in the functions they calculate. By a function f we mean a pairing of each number n with a unique number $f(n)$—called the value of f at n—usually specified by an algebraic formula (for simplicity, all our numbers will be natural numbers). For example, $f(n) = n^2 + n + 41$ defines a function which pairs off 1 with 43 ($= 1^2 + 1 + 41$), 2 with 47 ($= 2^2 + 2 + 41$), and so on. (Actually, the first thirty-nine values of this function are prime numbers, but this is beside the point.)

We may also define a function using words, and stipulate for example that $p(n)$ is the number of primes smaller than or equal to n. We then have $p(7) = 4$—as can be easily checked—and $p(4 \times 10^{16})$ = 1,075,292,778,753,150—as may be less easily verified. The calculation of both $f(n)$ and $p(n)$ can certainly be carried out on a computer, and since these machines were invented to help scientists with number-crunching, it is hardly surprising that they can also calculate much more complex functions. But can they compute any function whatsoever? This question is not just academic, because the

51

problem-solving capability of computers depends on the class of functions they can actually calculate.

It was Alan Turing who answered the above question in 1936, almost ten years before the birth of the world's first electronic computer—the Electronic Integrator and Calculator (ENIAC)—at the Moore School of Engineering in Philadelphia. At the time, Turing was not really concerned with practical devices such as computing machines, although after the war he worked on the development of an electronic computer. His paper on "computable numbers"[2] was intended as a solution to a mathematical problem posed by one of the most respected mathematicians of the century. But Turing's paper also showed that there are limits to automatic calculation, a kind of "natural law" which not even the most powerful present-day digital computers can escape.

Each time we solve a problem on a computer, the machine transforms the problem's data into the solution by executing a set of instructions or program. In the final analysis, both the data and the solution are strings of 0s and 1s that we may interpret as encoding natural numbers—possibly very large ones. Thus, from a conceptual point of view, computer programs are recipes for computing functions, since their execution transforms natural numbers (the input) into other natural numbers (the output). It is in this sense that questions about which problems computers can solve depend ultimately on the kind of functions they can compute.

TURING AND HIS MACHINES

Let us imagine the operations performed by the
computer to be split up into "simple operations" which
are so elementary that it is not easy to imagine them
further divided.
(*Alan Turing, analyzing the way a human computer carries
out a calculation*)[3]

In the summer of 1935, Alan Turing, then a young Cambridge graduate, was reflecting on a question in the foundations of mathematics that had been raised a few years earlier by the eminent German mathematician David Hilbert. Is there a mechanical test or process which, applied to an arbitrary mathematical statement, would permit one to discover whether the statement is true or false? Anyone attempting to answer this question had first to elucidate the hazy but fundamental notion of "mechanical process." This led Turing to ask himself what would be the most general kind of "machine" that could deal with symbols used by a person calculating with paper and pencil, but without the characteristically human faculties: cleverness, insight, imagination, and so forth—and also without the not less human weaknesses such as fatigue, hunger, or boredom.

"Computing is normally done by writing certain symbols on paper," wrote Turing.[4] "We may suppose this paper is divided into squares like a child's arithmetic book. In elementary arithmetic the two-dimensional character of the paper is sometimes used. But such a use is always avoidable, and I think that it will be agreed that the two-dimensional character of paper is no essential of computation. I assume then that the computation is carried out on one-dimensional paper, i.e., on a tape divided into squares. I shall also suppose that the number of symbols which may be printed is finite."

Turing had in mind an ideal device which could manipulate certain symbols (recognize them, write them down, erase them, etc.) and whose behavior would be automatic, that is, completely determined in advance. A few months later he came up with the idea of a simple theoretical model of a computer, known today as a Turing machine. He had also found the answer to Hilbert's question, but that is part of a different story, whose thread we shall pick up later.

Unlike actual computers, Turing's ideal machines can work unhindered by limitations of either time or memory space. They provide a standard (and precise) test for the intuitive notion of "computability": a function f will be called computable if each of its values $f(n)$ can be generated by the "mechanical" operations of some Turing machine.

We may imagine a Turing machine (TM) as composed of a read/write head and a two-dimensional tape that it uses as a writing pad (see fig. II.1). The tape extends indefinitely in both directions and is divided up into cells which may contain one of the two symbols 0 or 1 (it is convenient to think of 0 as representing a blank, or empty, cell). At any given stage in the computation, the head is scanning one of the cells and can do only one of the following four things: write a 1 (or a 0) on the cell (thus erasing the cell's former contents); move to the next cell on the right; or move to the next cell on the left. Which one of these actions takes place will depend on the machine's "pro-

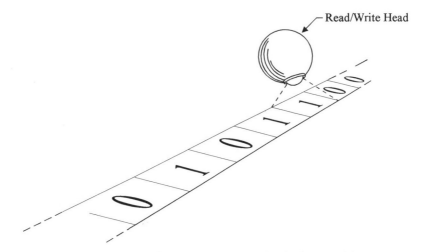

FIGURE II.1. A crude representation of a Turing machine.

gram"—the set of instructions the TM comes equipped with. These instructions must be written in a standard format. The following is an example:

#788: "If the symbol being scanned is 1, then move (one cell) to the left and then execute instruction #559."

The above instruction may be succinctly coded as (#788, 1, L, #559). In general, the format of a coded instruction is

(instruction no., [scanned] symbol, action, [next] instruction no.).

A program for a Turing machine is any set of instructions coded in this way (the order in which the instructions are listed is irrelevant). As a simple example, suppose that the program consists of the following five instructions:

$$(\#1, 1, R, \#2)$$
$$(\#2, 0, 1, \#2)$$
$$(\#2, 1, L, \#3)$$
$$(\#3, 0, 1, \#1)$$
$$(\#1, 0, 1, \#3).$$

When the machine is "turned on," there is a certain binary string (the data) written on its tape, and the head is scanning one of the cells. Let us assume that the machine is turned on scanning a 1, while the rest of the tape is blank. Then the following sequence of operations takes place. The first instruction to be executed is instruction #1. Notice that there are two instructions #1, but only one of them corresponds to the case where the symbol being scanned is 1. So this instruction—(#1, 1, R, #2)—is executed, causing the head to move one cell to the right and then to "go to #2," that is, execute (#2, 0, 1, #2), since the symbol now being scanned is 0. The execution of this instruction results in the 0 being replaced by 1 and then—again—"going to #2." The instruction matching the current situation is now (#2, 1, L, #3), so the head moves to the next cell on the left (which contains the initial 1) and then looks for instruction #3. But no instruction begins with (#3, 1, . . .), so the computation stops.

Of course, all this activity takes place only in a figurative sense. The whole process could have been phrased in mathematical language, but it is easier to imagine it in terms of a machine executing instructions. The final tape now contains two consecutive 1s—the rest of it has remained blank. Different tape configurations at the beginning of the computation will generally result in different tapes at the end. For instance, had the initial tape been totally blank, the head would have written a single 1 and then stopped.

In the course of a computation, a TM has an unlimited amount of cells to read, write, and store information. Digital computers, on the other hand, have only a fixed number of memory bits at their disposal for all their operations. And while real computers must deliver an output within a reasonable period of time, a Turing machine has no such time limit for giving its answer. Notice, however, that this answer—if answer there is—will come after some finite interval of time (T units of time, say, if the unit is chosen as the time required to execute one instruction), during which the head will have read (or written on) only a finite number (N) of cells. Both T and N can be arbitrary large numbers, but not infinity. Although ideal machines such as TMs could never be actually built, their study is important because it provides a kind of upper bound on the computing power of real ones.

COMPUTABLE FUNCTIONS

The reader should not be misled by the trivial example of a Turing machine given above, whose sole purpose was to illustrate the operations. Compared to present-day computers, TMs may appear very primitive indeed, so much so that even a modest PC seems considerably more powerful. However, as we shall soon see, there is much more to these "machines" than meets the eye of the mind. In particular, they are amazingly good at computing functions. How they do this is explained in the following paragraphs.

Suppose that each time we start up a particular TM with a number n written (in some conventional format) on its tape, the machine eventually halts, and when it does, the tape contains the number $f(n)$ (encoded in the conventional format). In that case we say that the Turing machine in question computes the function $f(n)$. For instance, if a TM takes as input a block of n consecutive 1s and doubles it—that is, its output tape contains a block of $2n$ consecutive 1s—we may say that the machine computes the function $f(n) = 2n$. Any function that can be computed by some Turing machine will be called computable. This is such an important definition that it is worth stating again:

A function of natural numbers is said to be computable if it can be computed by some Turing machine.

In order to make this definition totally unambiguous we ought to specify several things: how to encode the input data on the tape, which cell the head should be scanning when the computation begins, and so on. There are many sensible ways of doing all this, but the actual choice of a computation protocol is unimportant because it turns out that exactly the same functions are computable whichever (reasonable) scheme is adopted. What *is* important is to realize that once a particular protocol is chosen, every Turing machine computes a unique function.

It is quite possible that for certain inputs a given TM may never terminate its computation, and even if it does, more often than not there will be a meaningless string of symbols written on its final tape. In either case, we say that the function computed by the machine is not defined for the given input data. Hence, the functions computed by Turing machines are in general partial functions—functions f that do not assign any value $f(n)$ to some numbers n.

It can be argued, as Turing himself did, that the notion of a Turing machine captures the essential features of our intuitive idea of "mechanical procedure" or "algorithm." If we accept this fact, then to show that a function f is computable it is enough to describe a

56

procedure for calculating $f(n)$ that is "mechanical" in an intuitive sense—since such a method could then be coded as the set of instructions for a TM. Here is an example. In any circle, the ratio of the circumference to the diameter is the famous number π ($=$ pi $=$ 3.14159...). Let $f(n)$ be the nth decimal of π, that is, $f(1) = 1$, $f(2) = 4$, $f(5) = 9$, and so forth. Now, π is an irrational number, which means that its decimals do not obey any discernible pattern. There are, however, several algorithms which systematically calculate the decimals of π, one after the other. Then, to compute, say, $f(1,000,000)$, we can run one of these algorithms until it prints out the one-millionth decimal. Since such a procedure "mechanically" calculates $f(n)$ for an arbitrary n, f is computable.

Now consider another function, g, which is a partial function because it is defined only for n ranging from 1 to 9. By definition, $g(n) = 1$ if there is a block of n consecutive digits "n" in the decimal part of π; if no such block exists, then $g(n) = 0$. For example, it is obvious that $g(1) = 1$—there *is* one "1" (actually, the first decimal); $g(2)$ is either 1 or 0; it is 1 if somewhere in the decimal part of π there is a block of two consecutive "2"s, that is, if $\pi = 3,14159...22...$ But if no "22" block exists, then $g(2) = 0$.

Is g computable or not? We might try to compute g by running the algorithm that calculates f, but there is a problem. To compute, say, $g(4)$, we must find out whether or not the block "4444" appears in the decimal part of π. Now, if there is such a block, we will eventually know it, for the algorithm will print it out sooner or later; but if no "4444" block exists, the algorithm will be searching forever and the computation of $g(4)$ will never be completed. Hence, we cannot a priori guarantee that our method will calculate $g(n)$ for every n *in a finite period of time*, so we are unable to settle the question of the computability of g with the above approach. It turns out that g is computable after all, and we challenge the interested reader to prove it. As for the impatient reader, he or she can turn right away to the section Solution to the Riddle.

UNCOMPUTABLE FUNCTIONS

All functions defined by an explicit formula involving the operations of addition, multiplication, and exponentiation are computable, for example $f(n) = n^3 + 4n^2 + 1$ and $g(n) = (n + 10)^n$. (There are some technical problems with subtraction and division, since we are restricting ourselves to natural numbers, but these problems can be overcome.) Functions specified by recursion schemes, which use previously calculated values to compute the new value $f(n)$, also turn out to be computable. A famous example is the sequence $1, 1, 2, 3, 5, 8, 13, \ldots$ which the thirteenth-century Italian mathematician Leonardo Fibonacci introduced while studying the way rabbits breed. The Fibonacci sequence starts off with two consecutive 1s, and then each successive entry is the sum of the two preceding ones. In symbols:

$$f(1) = 1; \quad f(2) = 1 \quad \text{and} \quad f(n) = f(n-1) + f(n-2), \quad \text{for } n \geq 3.$$

Thus, $f(3) = f(2) + f(1) = 2$; $f(4) = f(3) + f(2) = 3$, and so forth.

As a matter of fact, every function a non-mathematician might ever come across is likely to be computable. But are *all* functions computable? Is "computable function" a pleonasm? A simple logical argument will show the answer to these questions to be negative.

Remember that each TM comes with its own program, that is, it is wired up once and for all to obey a certain set of instructions. If we wish to run a different program we need a new machine (this is nothing more than a convention and it is certainly not a waste of "machines"). A consequence of this convention is that each Turing machine computes a single function. But is every function computed by *some* Turing machine?

Even though there are infinitely many TMs, we can arrange them all on a (virtual) list. For instance, since a TM is completely specified by a finite string of symbols—its program—we could (at least in principle) list all TMs by systematically enumerating all possible programs $P_1, P_2, P_3, \ldots$ in some kind of alphabetical order. (If A is a finite set of symbols, say $A = \{a, b, c\}$, then the finite strings of symbols from A can be arranged "alphabetically" on an infinite list: $a, b, c, aa, ab, ac, ba, bb, bc, ca, cb, cc, aaa, aab, \ldots$ etc.)

On the other hand, the functions of natural numbers cannot be all written down on a list, not even in principle. This impossibility may be proved by an ingenious mathematical argument. The gist of the argument goes like this: You give me a list of functions and I show you a function that is not on your list; hence, your list is incomplete (for the full argument, see Appendix 2). The bottom line is that there are more functions than Turing machines to compute them or, in short, that there exist uncomputable functions.

The reader might be mystified by our having resorted to indirect evidence in order to establish the existence of uncomputable functions. Wouldn't it have been easier—and certainly much more illuminating—to exhibit one such function? The problem is, uncomputable functions are not easy to either define or discover. And even if we should happen to meet one, it might be hard to prove that the function is not computable, just as hard as proving that certain problems have no solution. In fact, the two questions are intimately related.

An Unsolvable Problem

Since there exist uncomputable functions, we should expect that Turing machines would be unable to solve certain problems. It is of course possible that all such unsolvable problems be merely theoretical curiosities, of no practical interest whatsoever. In reality, one of the questions that TMs cannot answer is very practical indeed because it concerns the automatic checking of computer software: it is the question of deciding whether the execution of an arbitrary computer program will eventually terminate or is doomed to run forever.

As we have already pointed out, certain Turing machines may never stop computing. For a trivial example, consider the TM whose only instruction is $(\#1, 0, R, \#1)$. If the initial tape is blank, this machine will keep executing its single instruction forever, thus perpetually moving its head to the next cell on the right along its infinite tape (someone once called it a "touring" machine). Imagine now an arbitrary Turing machine, controlled perhaps by thousands of instructions. Would it be possible to predict whether or not its computation will ever halt? This puzzle is known as the halting problem. It consists in finding a way of (correctly) answering yes or no to the following question: Will Turing machine T, if started on a given input tape, eventually terminate its computation?

In concrete terms, suppose we were looking for a "device" (machine, crystal ball, oracle, or what have you) capable of giving the correct answer to the above question for all Turing machines T. While such a thing might well exist, it cannot be a Turing machine. In other words, it is impossible to write a program for a Turing machine—H, say—that would perform as follows: *H* accepts as input the set of instructions of an arbitrary Turing machine *T* together with the contents of its initial tape (all these data encoded in some convenient way) and it produces as output "yes" if *T* will eventually halt and "no" if *T* will keep running forever. That is, *H* is capable of predicting whether or not any given Turing machine would ever stop computing.

Alas, *H* cannot exist. If it did, it would lead to a logical contradiction (see Appendix 3 for details). And so, whatever it takes to tell apart the TMs that terminate their computation from those that don't, this cannot be done on a Turing machine. In a nutshell: The halting problem is unsolvable on any Turing machine.

THE ANT, THE BULLDOZER, AND THE LIMITS OF COMPUTABILITY

Computers are formidable calculators, with their superfast parallel processors, random-access memories, and so forth. By comparison, Turing machines, chugging along one cell at a time, appear as models of inefficiency (they can afford to be inefficient, disposing as they do of inexhaustible resources—time, paper, ink, etc.). Consequently, the fact that some functions cannot be computed by Turing machines may not seem to be a serious limitation, for it is conceivable that those functions could be computed by other, more powerful calculating devices.

Perhaps so, but whatever these "devices" might be, they cannot resemble our familiar computers. For all their imposing power and speed, digital computers are in fact glorified Turing machines—with the added disadvantage of space and time constraints. The reason for this humbling of digital computers is quite simple: since their workings fit the description of "mechanical procedure," they can be simulated on a Turing machine. To be sure, the modest TM may have to execute thousands of very elementary operations to perform even a simple multiplication. In the end, however, the output will be the same, whether efficiently computed by the real machine or laboriously calculated by the ideal one. It's like moving a pile of sand from one place to another. A single ant, carrying one grain at a time, can in principle accomplish the task as surely as a mighty bulldozer. Thus, everything a computer can do could also be done on a TM. Which leads to an inescapable conclusion: those functions that no Turing machine can compute remain uncomputable on any real digital computer—present or future.

Besides Turing's, other definitions have been proposed seeking to render mathematically precise the intuitive idea of a computation. It turns out, however, that they are all equivalent, that is, regardless of which one we adopted the set of computable functions would be exactly the same. This state of affairs prompted the American logician Alonzo Church to state what is known as Church's Thesis: All functions computable in an intuitive sense are computable on a Turing machine.

Church, a professor at Princeton University, had been working on Hilbert's question at about the same time as the solitary Turing. Using quite different methods, and each ignoring the other's efforts, both mathematicians arrived at the answer almost simultaneously on opposite sides of the Atlantic. What Church called "effectively calculable" corresponded to Turing's notion of "computable"—that is, anything that can be computed by a Turing machine. Some years later though, the former "rivals" were to work together at Princeton.

To this day, Church's Thesis stands, for no one has found a function that can be reasonably called "computable" and which demonstrably cannot be computed by any Turing machine. If Church's conjecture is correct—and the evidence so far suggests that it is—then the functions no Turing machine can compute are also uncomputable in an absolute sense.

Lifting the Veil over Uncomputable Functions

Uncomputable functions are not something occult, too mysterious for the uninitiated to contemplate. It is rather a question of knowing where to find them. A sure way of bumping into one is by trying to "compute" the solution of some problem no Turing machine can solve. We already know one puzzle of this kind: that of testing whether an arbitrary Turing machine will ever stop computing (the halting problem). It is now simply a matter of translating the halting question into the language of functions.

Present-day communication technology is based on the digitalization of information, the encoding of text, images, and sounds as strings of 0s and 1s on some suitable support (diskette, CD, etc.). The process is of course reversible, for we can recover the text or sound from its coded form (by reading the diskette or playing the CD). In addition, the encoding/decoding is totally automatic, since it is performed by machines.

In a similar fashion, it is in principle possible to automatically encode the program of any given Turing machine as a single natural number. This can be done, for example, by first converting each of the symbols needed to write Turing machine programs into a two-numeral code. Here is a possible conversion table:

$$
\begin{array}{ll}
0 = 00 & L = 10 \\
1 = 01 & R = 11 \\
2 = 02 & (= 12 \\
\ldots &) = 13 \\
9 = 09 & \# = 14 \\
& , = 15.
\end{array}
$$

Then, given a program P for a Turing machine, we can obtain a natural number by replacing the symbols (in the order they appear in P) by their two-numeral codes and finally reading the resulting string as a decimal number. Thus, the one-instruction program $(\#1, 0, R, \#1)$ becomes the number 1,214,011,500,151,115,140,113. (We are not claiming that the above encoding scheme is the most efficient one.)

It should be clear that the original program can be recovered from its code number by an appropriate (automatic) decoding. Notice that while every TM has a corresponding number (its program's code number), some natural numbers k may not encode any program—that is, decoding k would either yield a meaningless string of symbols or no string at all, anything but the program of a Turing machine. For instance, 1,110,071,212 decodes as RL7(((meaningless), while 789,999,555,333 does not decode at all. If a number m does happen to be the code number of a Turing machine, we shall designate this machine by $T(m)$.

We now define the function h of two variables as follows: for a given pair (m, n) of natural numbers, $h(m, n) = 1$, if m is the code of a Turing machine and this machine—$T(m)$—eventually halts after being started with the number n on its input tape. In all other cases —that is, if either m is not the code of a Turing machine or $T(m)$ does exist but it will never stop computing on input n—we set $h(m, n) = 0$.

Once again: $h(m, n) = 1$ if $T(m)$ exists and would eventually stop if started on input n, and $h(m, n) = 0$ otherwise.

How can we be sure that no Turing machine computes h? Because, as we show in Appendix 3, the assumption that a Turing machine does compute h leads straight to a logical contradiction. This method of proof by *reductio ad absurdum* (the reduction of a supposition to an absurdity) is one of the mathematician's best allies.

COMPLEXITY

Turing's results put a theoretical limit on what his ideal machines—and, a fortiori, real computers—can calculate. But, as extensive experimental evidence has shown, within those limits there is ample room for computing the solutions to all kinds of problems. The real question is rather how to actually get done, in an efficient way, the many things that digital computers are capable of doing. Unlike real computers, Turing machines have an unlimited amount of both time and memory space to compute their answers. And so, even if a problem is solvable on some Turing machine, there is no guarantee that the problem can be actually solved on a computer—if, for instance, the answer should take thousands of years to work out.

Mathematicians and computer scientists studying the practical aspects of computing have accumulated a rich body of theoretical and empirical results, loosely known as the theory of computational complexity. In particular, they have attempted to elucidate just what makes some problems harder to solve than others. To illustrate the main concepts of this field we shall employ a famous puzzle that has been called—arguably, with some exaggeration—the mother of all optimization problems.

OPTIMIZATION PROBLEMS

Anyone wishing to find the most efficient way of doing something may be facing what mathematicians call an optimization problem. Often, this means having to decide which is the best of a large number of strategies or alternatives. In a typical commercial or industrial situation, for example, the "best" option is usually the most economical one. Formally, for each alternative x there is an associated cost $c(x)$, and the problem then consists in finding an x for which $c(x)$ is as small as possible, that is, an optimal solution. Setting up itineraries for delivering goods and planning the production of a manufacturing plant are examples of large-scale optimization problems. In such cases, poor optimization can have devastating economic effects, hence the practical interest in the development of efficient solution methods. Some of these techniques proceed to calculate the optimal solution directly from the data (e.g., using differential calculus); other methods try to construct it step by step, beginning with some approximate solution and gradually improving it.

Solution techniques based on new computing paradigms offer some promising alternatives. For instance, genetic algorithms, which we shall introduce in chapter 6, work with a pool, or "population," of potential solutions whose composition is periodically updated by a mechanism that involves an element of chance. The long-term goal of this "evolutionary" process, which resembles natural selection, is to improve the average quality of future "generations" of solutions. If the updating operations are suitably chosen, there is a high probability that an exceptional individual—an optimal or near-optimal solution—will eventually appear.

One particular optimization problem has baffled some of the best mathematicians and computer scientists for a long time, and it is further evidence that an innocent-looking question can give rise to a very hard problem. In its original version, the question is about a sales representative who has to visit a number of cities. Beginning at some city, the sales rep must travel to each of the others once before returning to the starting point. In which order should the salesman visit the various cities so that the tour is as short as possible? Such is the puzzle known as the traveling salesman problem.

It sounds simple. All the traveling rep has to do is add the intercity distances for each possible tour and then choose the circuit with the smallest length. For example, a tour of six cities can be scheduled in 120 ways. This is the number $5 \times 4 \times 3 \times 2 \times 1$ of the different orderings, or permutations, of five objects. (Why five and not six? Because all tours must begin at the city where the sales rep lives, so this city need not be counted.) A computer will take only a fraction of a second to calculate the different tour lengths and pick out the shortest. Such is indeed a solution method, but one which is useless if the number of cities is, say, a mere fifty. For then an exhaustive, case-by-case calculation of each tour's length would involve so many operations that even the world's fastest supercomputer would take billions of years to work out the answer.

Not many real sales reps may have to visit fifty cities, but the problem also arises in industry and management, where good solutions might translate into considerable savings. In the manufacture of circuit boards, for example, lasers must drill tens of thousands of holes. The board "travels" around a fixed laser beam, and finding the sequence which takes the least time to drill is the traveling salesman problem in disguise. Other industrial applications—to VLSI chip fabrication, for instance—may involve millions of "cities."

Manfred Padberg, of the Leonard N. Stern School of Business at New York University is an expert in the sales rep puzzle. He observed that most of the techniques for the solution of hard combinatorial problems have been thought of, developed for, and tried out on the traveling salesman problem. According to AT & T Laboratories' David Johnson, another traveling salesman buff, the problem's appeal may be explained by its simplicity and applicability, or perhaps simply because of its intriguing name.

But the fascination with the traveling salesman may also stem from the fact that it is typical of a large class of hard problems that are computationally equivalent. This means that any efficient solution method for one particular problem in the class could be used to construct efficient algorithms for each of the others. Here "efficient" has a precise meaning, to be explained shortly.

PROBLEM SIZE

There is a distinction to be made between the general problem and the instances of the problem. Every time we specify a set of cities and the distances between them we have an instance of the traveling salesman problem. We may well succeed in finding the shortest tour for that particular instance, but to solve *the* problem we need a method that would lead to the solution of every instance, and do so in a reasonable time. The time condition is crucial for obvious practical reasons (who can wait thousands of years for the answer?). Naturally, we should expect the computation time to increase with the number of cities involved, that is, with the "size" of the instance.

The notions of problem size and reasonable running time need clarification.

The size of (a given instance of) a problem is the amount of computer memory needed to specify the data (measured in some appropriate unit such as bytes). For a traveling salesman problem, the data are the distances between each pair of cities, but for simplicity we shall take its size to be the number n of cities. Thus, a problem involving 48 cities has size 48. In general, the larger the size, the longer any given solution algorithm will take to give an answer—although computation time may also depend on other factors, such as the distribution of the cities.

The reason why the straightforward approach (computing all possible tour lengths) is unworkable may be understood with a simple example. For $n = 5$ cities, there are 24 possible tours; if the number of cities is increased 10 times to $n = 50$, the number of tours explodes to approximately 6×10^{62}, that is, an increase by a factor exceeding one quintillion times one quintillion (= 1 followed by 60 zeros)! Since the number of possibilities grows extremely fast with respect to problem size, the systematic checking of all tours in search of the optimal one soon becomes impossible. For a solution method to be feasible, the computational demands should not increase too rapidly with the size of the instance. Experts who studied the performance of algorithms have devised a classification of problems based on the mathematical relationship between, on the one hand, the size of the problem and, on the other, the number of computer operations needed to find a solution. The most popular class is known as P, or, more familiarly, as the class of easy problems.

POLYNOMIAL TIME

To estimate the efficiency of an algorithm it is customary to use either its running time on a computer or the number of elementary machine operations needed to execute it. But a satisfactory measure of efficiency should not depend on the particular computer chosen to run the algorithm. One way to obtain a uniform measure is to require that the algorithm be written as a program for a Turing machine. The notion of "operation" would then be perfectly clear—remember that a TM performs only three types of operation: move right, move left, and write a symbol. Moreover, by stipulating that the execution of an operation should take one unit of machine time, the same number would evaluate the number of operations and the running time. While such a theoretical detour via Turing machines would render our definitions totally precise, it would be extremely awkward to actually carry it out. Fortunately, there exist certain practical short-cuts. But first we must make a detour through college algebra.

The polynomials (in one variable x) are the functions obtained by performing the operations of addition and multiplication on x and on certain (constant) numbers $a_n, a_{n-1}, \ldots, a_1, a_0$. Consider, for example, the following sequence of operations: multiply x by itself (this gives x^2), then multiply by 3 (we now have $3x^2$), add x [$3x^2 + x$], multiply by 2 [$(3x^2 + x)2$], multiply by x [$(3x^2 + x)2x$], and finally add -5 to get the polynomial function $p(x) = (3x^2 + x)2x - 5$. Polynomials are the simplest type of function because their calculation involves only the simplest operations: addition and multiplication. Using properties of these two operations one can then show that a polynomial function may always be written in the standard form $p(x) = a_n x^n + a_{n-1} x^{n-1} + \cdots + a_1 x + a_0$, with a_n not equal to zero. The positive integer n is called the degree of the polynomial. The standard form of the polynomial in our example is $p(x) = 6x^3 + 2x^2 + 0x - 5$, and so this polynomial has degree 3. The class of polynomial functions has many pleasant algebraic properties. Not the least, the fact that another polynomial results from the addition or the multiplication of two polynomials, and also from taking the polynomial of a polynomial (obtained by replacing throughout the 'x' in $p(x)$ with another polynomial $q(x)$).

In general, it is not possible to calculate exactly how many operations an algorithm necessitates to solve a given problem of size n. The best we can usually do is estimate an upper bound $u(n)$ on the number of operations required to solve an arbitrary instance of size n —that is, we can guarantee that the number of operations will not exceed $u(n)$. This function $u(n)$, which normally increases with n, then becomes an approximate measure of how rapidly running time grows with problem size. If $u(n)$ is a polynomial function, we say that the given algorithm solves the problem "in polynomial time" (the algorithm itself is informally referred to as a polynomial time algorithm). In the hierarchy of rates of growth, polynomial occupies

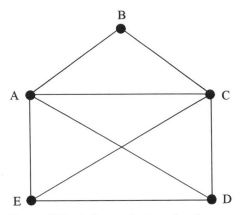

FIGURE II.2. A figure that can be drawn without lifting the pencil or tracing the same line twice.

the lowest level, just below exponential, which is the typical growth rate of bacterial cultures and outstanding debts.

A problem is in class P (as in Polynomial) if there is an algorithm which can solve it in polynomial time, or, more explicitly, if there is a polynomial $p(x)$ and an algorithm that can solve any instance of size n in less than $p(n)$ operations. One example is the Eulerian path problem, named after the eighteenth-century Swiss mathematical genius Leonhard Euler. In a popular version of the problem, a person is challenged to draw a certain figure without lifting the pencil or tracing the same line twice. For the picture in figure II.2, the following sequence of segments is one solution to the problem: *EA, AB, BC, CD, DE, EC, CA, AD*. But if the figure does not satisfy a certain condition (to be explained soon), the person may spend hours trying unsuccessfully to meet the challenge. The moral of the story: when solving a problem, keep in mind that it might not have a solution.

Mathematically, the Eulerian path problem consists in deciding whether or not a given graph has a path that visits each "edge" exactly once (a Eulerian path). A graph with m "vertices" may be represented as an $m \times m$ binary matrix, or square array of 0s and 1s. If we number the vertices from 1 to m, then the entry in the i-th row and j-th column will be 1 in case vertices i and j are joined by an edge, and it will be 0 if they are not. Labeling the vertices of the graph in figure II.2 with numbers $1, 2, \ldots, 5$, instead of the letters $A, B, \ldots, E$, results in the following matrix:

$$
\begin{array}{ccccc}
0 & 1 & 1 & 1 & 1 \\
1 & 0 & 1 & 0 & 0 \\
1 & 1 & 0 & 1 & 1 \\
1 & 0 & 1 & 0 & 1 \\
1 & 0 & 1 & 1 & 0.
\end{array}
$$

Under this representation, the size of the problem is m^2 (the number of entries in the matrix). How can we decide, based solely on the above binary matrix, whether or not there is a Eulerian path? Mathematics comes to our rescue. Let us call "degree" of a vertex the number of edges that meet at that vertex. For example, in the above graph, A has degree 4 and E has degree 3. Notice that the degree of vertex i is equal to the number of 1s in the i-th row of the matrix. Now, as Euler showed, a graph G has a Eulerian path precisely if the number of its vertices of odd degree is either 0 or 2. In the first case, G has a Eulerian closed path (one that begins and ends at the same vertex); in the second, the Eulerian path begins at one odd degree vertex and ends at the other. The proof of Euler's theorem is not really difficult, but it is not necessary for our purposes.

One algorithm to decide the Eulerian path question checks the parity of each row of the matrix—that is, whether the number of 1s is even or odd—and keeps a record of the number of rows with odd parity. If the final count is either 0 or 2, then the answer (to the decision question) will be yes, otherwise, it will be no. A rough estimate reveals that the procedure just outlined involves less than $2m^2 + 3$ computational steps. Thus, the polynomial $p(n) = 2n + 3$ in the size $n\, (= m^2)$ of the instance is an upper bound on the number of operations required to solve the problem, and so it is a polynomial time computation.

Another class P problem is that of finding the shortest routes from a given city to each of n other cities, because it can be shown that a particular algorithm for solving this problem requires less than $p(n) = n^3$ operations. Assuming a modest computational speed of 1,024 $(= 2^{10})$ operations per second, this algorithm would take less than half an hour to solve any problem involving 128 cities ($n = 128$). Let us compare this performance with that of an exponential time algorithm, one that delivers a solution of the shortest routes problem after 2^n (instead of n^3) operations. For the same number (128) of cities, such an algorithm would require a mind-boggling 10^{19} billion years to work out the answer. And even with a speed of computation one billion times faster, the solution would still take a prohibitive 10^{10} billion years to calculate.

The above example may help explain why exponential time algorithms are, save some notable exceptions, useless for all practical purposes. And also why problems whose solutions depend on such algorithms are generally considered to be intractable, and will remain so in the foreseeable future—even allowing for the (realistic) development of faster computers. By contrast, class P problems are usually tractable, and their polynomial time algorithms (which are normally of low degree) have been nicknamed "efficient" algorithms. Is the traveling salesman a class P problem? The simple truth is, we don't know. No one has yet found an "efficient" solution, that is, an algorithm that computes the shortest tour of n cities in polynomial time—but neither has anyone shown that such an algorithm does not exist.

THE NP CLASS

A second class of problems is known by the inelegant name of nondeterministic polynomial time verifiable—NP for short. Strictly speaking, the label NP only applies to decision problems, or problems requiring a yes or no answer. But since almost any problem may be cast as a closely related decision problem, the distinction is often blurred. In the case of the traveling salesman, instead of asking for the shortest tour we could ask: Is there a tour whose length is K or less? (where K is some positive integer). There is no more a known polynomial time algorithm to solve this problem than there is one to solve the original version, but formulating it as a decision problem allows us to separate the search for a solution into two stages. In the first stage, a possible solution (a particular list S of cities) is "guessed," while the second stage "verifies" whether or not S is indeed a solution—a tour of length K or less.

The (decision) problems in NP may be roughly described as those whose solutions might be difficult to find but are easy to check. More precisely, a problem is in NP if the verification of any solution candidate can be done in polynomial time (on the problem size). It is precisely this idea of polynomial time "verifiability" that the class of NP problems is intended to capture.

What about the "nondeterministic" bit, that is, the N in NP? A precise definition of the NP class involves the notion of a nondeterministic Turing machine (NDTM), whose role is to do the "guessing" of potential solutions. We may imagine a NDTM as composed of a write-only head. When turned on, the head writes an arbitrary binary string on its tape. At each stage of the operation, the machine "chooses" in a nondeterministic (i.e., in a random) manner whether to write a 0, a 1, or to stop writing altogether. When—and if—the head chooses to stop, the binary string on its tape is passed on to an ordinary Turing machine which then begins the verification process in the usual (deterministic) way. This ordinary TM has been provided beforehand with the relevant data concerning the particular instance of the decision problem being solved (the intercity distances, in the case of a traveling salesman problem). Thus, instead of carrying out just one computation per instance, the tandem NDTM-TM performs an infinite number of them, one for each possible guess. If for every yes-instance of the problem there is a correct guess and a computation that verifies it in polynomial time, we then say that the problem is in class NP. The decision problems in NP may therefore be informally defined as those that a nondeterministic Turing machine can solve in polynomial time.

As Michael Garey and David Johnson observe in *Computers and Intractability*,[5] the use of the term "solve" in this informal definition should be taken with a grain of salt, since "a 'polynomial time nondeterministic algorithm' is basically a definitional device for capturing the notion of polynomial time verifiability, rather than a realistic method for solving decision problems."

For a traveling salesman problem, the verification of a "guess" G begins by checking that G encodes a permutation, or tour T, of the cities, followed (in case G does encode a tour) by the calculation of the length L of T and finally by comparing L with the bound K. It should be clear that this "verification" stage could be specified as a polynomial time algorithm, and hence that the (decision version of the) traveling salesman puzzle is in NP.

WILL A REAL HARD PROBLEM IN NP PLEASE STAND UP?

Every decision problem in P is automatically in NP. The reason is simply that any deterministic polynomial time algorithm (or Turing machine) qualifies as a nondeterministic one—for, in effect, it can afford to bypass the guessing stage and move right on to answering (yes or no) the decision question. It seems reasonable to expect that the NP class, having a different name and a more involved definition, should be distinct from (and therefore larger than) the class P. In other words, that there are problems in NP which are not already in P. But is it actually the case that P ≠ NP?

It will perhaps comfort the reader to learn that he or she is no more ignorant on this matter than the army of experts who have been pondering the question for decades. All efforts at proving P ≠ NP have so far failed, but no one has shown that P = NP either. Some fairly reputable computer scientists have thought to have settled the question, only to retract when errors in their proposed proofs were discovered. There is a widespread belief among complexity specialists that P is smaller than NP. Consequently, they have long been operating under the assumption that there exist problems in NP that are not in P—"hard" problems. Those working in complexity theory, not unlike theologians, cannot be blamed for having faith in the existence of their prime object of study.

To render the situation even more intriguing, the empirical evidence for and against P ≠ NP appears to cancel out. On the one hand, the failure of a considerable amount of effort to prove P ≠ NP would strongly suggest that the result is false. But then, how come no one has yet found a polynomial time solution (so sought after, for practical reasons) of any famous problem in NP, including the traveling salesman? So, appropriately, life is not simple in the universe of complexity. But computer theorists are very resourceful, and, short of showing the existence of hard NP problems, they have devised a test to establish that some problems in NP are the "hardest" to solve.

NP-Completeness

The term "NP-complete" has come to symbolize the
abyss of inherent intractability that algorithm designers
increasingly face as they seek to solve larger and more
complex problems.
(Michael R. Garey and David S. Johnson)[6]

In 1971, Stephen Cook, a professor at the University of Toronto,
showed that a particular decision problem in formal logic could
qualify as the "hardest" problem in NP. Cook also identified for the
first time the classes P and NP, although the idea of a polynomial
time algorithm can be traced back to Edmonds in the mid 1960s, who
informally called them "good algorithms." Edmonds[7] also introduced
a notion analogous to NP, that of problems having solutions that
admit "proofs" verifiable in polynomial time.

Cook's problem is known as the satisfiability problem, or SAT. An
instance of SAT is a logical formula, or Boolean expression, such as

$[x_1$ or x_3 or $x_5]$ and $[x_4$ or x_1 or (not $x_5)]$ and $[($not $x_4)$ or (not $x_2)$
or (not $x_3)]$,

where $x_1, x_2, \ldots, x_5$ represent Boolean variables which may take one
of the two truth values: 0 (= false) or 1 (= true). The (decision)
question to be answered is whether there exists an assignment of
truth values to the variables that makes the expression true ("satisfies" it). We remind the reader that "x or y" is true if one of x, y is
true; "x and y" is true if both x, y are true; and "not x" is true if x
is false. Then, for the following assignment, the above expression is
true: $x_1 = x_3 = x_4 = x_5 = 1$; $x_2 = 0$. And so, in this particular case,
we can easily answer the decision question—but then, very small
instances of hard problems always seem deceivingly simple to solve.

A general instance of SAT consists of a finite set D of disjunctions,
each of these involving three variables and/or their negations. A
simple example of a set D with four disjunctions is:

$[x_1$ or (not $x_3)$ or $x_5]$, $[x_4$ or x_1 or $x_5]$, $[($not $x_4)$ or (not $x_2)$ or (not
$x_3)]$, $[x_2$ or x_5 or (not $x_1)]$.

The question is then whether or not there exist an assignment of truth values to the variables appearing in D (there may be thousands of them) which simultaneously satisfies (i.e., makes true) all the disjunctions in the set.

Checking whether a given assignment of truth values satisfies a finite set of disjunctions is clearly a task that can be accomplished in polynomial time. Therefore, SAT is an NP problem. What Cook showed in his seminal theorem[8] (whose proof is rather complicated) is that SAT possesses the following additional "completeness" property: any instance of a problem in NP can be transformed, in polynomial time, into an instance of SAT; moreover, the answer to the decision question is the same for both of these instances. The bottom line is that if (a big if) SAT could somehow be "efficiently" solved (i.e., solved in polynomial time) then so could *every* problem in NP, and the distinction between "hard" and "easy"—between NP and P problems—would collapse, because NP would then be identical to P!

Problems having the above "completeness" property form a subclass of NP known as the NP-complete class. They include a wide variety of commonly encountered problems from mathematics and operations research, notably our famous traveling salesman. Determining the most probable arrangement of cloned fragments of a DNA sequence is an NP-complete problem in molecular biology. There are also NP-complete problems in practically every area of computer science, from sorting and searching to multiprocessor scheduling.

All the NP-complete problems share the property of being "the hardest problem in NP." This may be just an illusion: if P = NP, then all the NP problems believed to be "hard" could be solved in polynomial time and would not merit that label. But from a practical standpoint, knowing that a problem is NP-complete is a valuable piece of information, because it means that the chances of developing an efficient solution algorithm are next to nil. Unless, of course, two generations of computer scientists have been fooled by a mirage.

SOLUTION TO THE RIDDLE

We have already met (in the section Computable Functions) the function g, which was defined as $g(n) = 1$ if there is a block of n consecutive digits "n" in the decimal part of π, and $g(n) = 0$, if no such block exists. There we challenged the reader to prove that g is computable by some Turing machine. Here is the solution—or rather, *one* solution—to the riddle.

Notice that g takes either the value 0 or the value 1 for $n = 1, 2, \ldots, 9$ and it is undefined for all other natural numbers. There are exactly 512 ($= 2^9$) functions with those properties, and for each of them we could easily write the program of a Turing machine that computes it. Since g is computed by one of those 512 TMs, it is therefore computable. The peculiar thing about g is that we may not be able to tell *which* Turing machine computes it—I, for one, certainly can't. All we know for sure is that there *is* one Turing machine that computes g, which is all that is required by the definition of computable function.

NOTES

1. Georges Ifrah, *Histoire universelle des chiffres*, Laffont, 1994, vol. 2, p. 495.

2. A. M. Turing, "On Computable Numbers, with an Application to the Entscheidungsproblem," *Proc. of the London Mathematical Society*, ser. 2, vol. 42 (1936–37), pp. 230–65.

3. Ibid.

4. Ibid.

5. M. R. Garey and D. S. Johnson, *Computers and Intractability: A Guide to the Theory of NP-Completeness*, W. H. Freeman, San Francisco, 1979.

6. Ibid., preface.

7. J. Edmonds [1965], "Minimum Partition of a Matroid into Independent Subsets," *J. Res. Nat. Bur. Standards Sect.* B 69, 67–72.

8. S. A. Cook [1971], "The Complexity of Theorem-Proving Procedures," *Proc. 3rd. Ann. ACM Symp. on Theory of Computing*, Association for Computing Machinery, New York, 151–58.

CHAPTER FOUR

The Limits of Formal Reasoning

IN THE BEGINNING THERE WERE AXIOMS

THE PROBLEM of deciding whether the execution of an arbitrary computer program will eventually terminate cannot be solved on any Turing machine, as we have seen in the previous chapter. Although on the surface this result appears to concern only the theory of computing, it has unexpected implications reaching deep into the nature of mathematics itself. Such fundamental questions as "Can all mathematical problems be solved?" and "Is there a 'mechanical' test for mathematical truth?" are intimately related to the halting problem.

The search for mathematical wisdom begins with certain initial assumptions, or axioms, whose truth is taken for granted. Then, armed solely with pure logic and guided by their intuition, mathematicians proceed to derive other truths—the theorems. The great edifice of mathematics is thus constructed, theorem by theorem. Assuming a flawless logic, the soundness of the whole building is then a necessary consequence of the solidity of its foundations: if the axioms are true, so are the theorems. The Greek mathematician Euclid was the first to use this axiomatic approach some 2,300 years ago to develop geometry in a systematic way. Until recently, high school students could get a glimpse of this powerful method, most revealing of the deductive nature of mathematics, through the study of geometry from textbooks based on Euclid's masterpiece—the *Elements*. But geometry *à la* Euclid (and most of geometry itself) did not survive the sweeping changes in mathematics education of the 1970s. Ironically, those who designed the new math curricula had learned their mathematics the old-fashioned way, presumably with success.

The study of the natural numbers, or arithmetic, is perhaps the quintessential mathematical theory. Several axiom systems for arithmetic circulated at the beginning of this century, when questions about the foundations of mathematics were very popular among mathematicians and logicians. Typically, the axioms merely state certain obvious truths about the natural numbers, such as: each n has a successor $(n + 1)$, different numbers have different successors, and so on. Other systems may include as axioms the basic laws governing the familiar operations of addition and multiplication. Among these laws we find the commutative properties: $n + m = m + n$ and $nm = mn$, for all natural numbers n, m; the distributivity of multiplication over addition: $n(m + k) = nm + nk$, and so forth.

Every property of the natural numbers that can be logically inferred from the axioms is a theorem, and the totality of all (proven) theorems constitutes the reservoir of our present arithmetical knowledge.

PROBING THE FOUNDATIONS

The instrument which brings about the adjustment of
differences between theory and practice, between
thought and experiment, is mathematics. It builds the
connecting bridge and continually strengthens it. Thus
it happens that our entire present culture, insofar as it is
concerned with the intellectual understanding and
conquest of nature, rests upon mathematics!
(David Hilbert)[1]

Regardless of which statements we choose as axioms, two natural (for a logician) questions will insinuate themselves: Can a contradiction ever be deduced from the axioms?—this is known as the consistency question. And the question of completeness: Can all (arithmetical) truths be proved from the axioms? A particular axiom system (for arithmetic, or for some other branch of mathematics) is said to be consistent and complete if the answers to the above questions are, respectively, no and yes. To paraphrase the courtroom formula: the axioms are consistent and complete if we can logically deduce from them the whole truth (completeness) and nothing but the truth (consistency).

The question of consistency has haunted mathematicians and philosophers for a long time, and to this day there is no conclusive answer.[2] Of course, mathematicians feel deep in their hearts that arithmetic is consistent. In 1924, the distinguished German geometer Felix Klein presented the typical case for consistency: "Intuition shows us," he wrote, "the existence of numbers for which these laws hold [i.e., commutativity, distributivity, etc.] and it is consequently impossible for contradictions to lurk in these laws."[3]

But Klein's argument will not persuade the so-called formalists, who mistrust intuition and do not believe in the existence of the natural numbers, or of any other mathematical entities, for that matter. In the formalists' universe, the only reality is that of marks on paper—the expressions in a formal language—that can be manipulated according to specific rules. Since these formal expressions are not supposed to have any meaning, they are neither true nor false. On the altar of pure formalism, not just meaning but also the notion of truth is sacrificed.

Formalism is usually associated with the name of David Hilbert, who made capital contributions to mathematics and its foundations. But the famous German mathematician was in fact a firm believer in classical mathematics. The formal approach was for him only a strategical device to establish the soundness of the traditional methods of proof—especially those involving the concept of infinity —which were under attack by a dissident group known as the intuitionists. In 1928, Hilbert addressed the International Congress of Mathematicians in Bologna. He presented as central open questions the consistency and completeness of arithmetic, and also of larger systems such as classical mathematical analysis. There is little doubt that Hilbert expected these formal systems to be both consistent and complete.

A proof of consistency would have persuaded the skeptics that number theory and analysis, those pillars of the mathematical temple, were free from internal contradictions, thus guaranteeing that no incongruous proposition such as $2 + 2 = 5$ could ever be deduced. And establishing completeness would have confirmed, in Hilbert's words, "the conviction which every mathematician shares, although it has not yet been supported by proof" that every mathematical problem can be solved.[4] Hilbert was also convinced that our understanding and eventual conquest of nature rested upon mathematics; hence the importance he attached to validating its foundations. At the peak of his glory, even if retirement was nearing, how could he have suspected that his optimistic agenda would soon be bitterly frustrated?

FORMAL LANGUAGES

In order to better understand what is at stake here, let us go back to Euclid and his axiomatic method. When he wrote his famous *Elements* around 300 B.C., Euclid employed a natural language—Greek—to describe relations among geometrical objects (points, lines, etc.). But if we expect to answer questions about mathematics itself, such as "Is statement S a theorem?" we need to specify exactly what constitutes a mathematical statement. One way of doing this is by using a formal language. Examples of such languages are the programming languages used to write the instructions for a computer. A major difference between natural and formal languages is that the latter have very precise grammatical rules, allowing us (or a machine) to determine unambiguously which expressions in the language are meaningful statements.

A formal language suitable for writing about the natural numbers is the so-called language of arithmetic. Its alphabet consists of several types of symbols: The numerals 0 and 1; the letters $a, b, \ldots, x, y, z$—which represent arbitrary natural numbers; the operation symbols $+$ (for addition) and $\cdot$ (multiplication); the equality symbol ($=$), and the logical symbols $\neg$ (not), $\vee$ (or), $\&$ (and), $\Rightarrow$ (if...then), $\exists$ (for some), and $\forall$ (for all). The meaningful expressions of the language are strings of symbols from this alphabet formed according to certain precise rules of syntax—which would be too wearisome to specify here. Every (meaningful) expression "says something" about the natural numbers. For example,

$$\forall x(x + x = x \cdot x \Rightarrow (x = 0 \vee x = 1 + 1)) \tag{1}$$

reads, when translated into English: "If a number added to itself equals its square, then the number is either 0 or 2," while

$$\forall x((\neg\exists z(\neg(z = 1) \,\&\, \neg(z = x) \,\&\, \exists y(y \cdot z = x))$$

$$\Rightarrow \exists w(w + 1 + 1 + 1 = x)) \tag{2}$$

means: "Every prime number is greater than or equal to 3."

Familiarity with the formal language's syntactic rules is of course necessary to effect the translation. A literal translation of (2) would be: "For all (natural numbers) x, if it does not exist z such that z is not equal to 1 and z is not equal to x and, for some y, $y \cdot z = x$ [in other words, if no number other than 1 and x itself divides x—which is equivalent to 'if x is prime'] then there exists w such that $w + 3 = x$ [another way of saying 'then x is greater than or equal to 3']." This example illustrates one of the disadvantages of formal languages as a means of communication: sentences soon become much too long and hardly comprehensible.

A great deal of number theory can be couched in this formal language. Some statements, such as (1) above, are true (as can be easily checked by solving the equation $2x = x^2$), while others are false. Statement (2) is obviously false, for 2 is a prime number smaller than 3. To declare these two statements true and false, respectively, we have used our knowledge of the natural numbers and their operations. For most formal statements, however, a decision as to whether they are true or not would be much harder to come by. The jury is still out on such innocent-looking propositions as "Every even number greater than 2 is the sum of two primes," the so-called Goldbach conjecture. The assertion is true, for example, of the numbers 4 ($= 2 + 2$), 20 ($= 17 + 3$), 66 ($= 59 + 7$), and of many others. Actually, no one has yet found an even number that is not the sum of two primes; but nor has anyone demonstrated that such a number cannot exist, so the question is still unsettled. If we fail in our attempts to discover whether a given statement is true or false, someone more knowledgeable or more ingenious may succeed. Could this "someone" be a machine?

MECHANICAL MATHEMATICS

In his famous 1928 address to the mathematical community, David Hilbert had also asked whether mathematics was decidable. By this he understood: Is there a definite method, akin to a "mechanical" procedure, which when applied to an arbitrary mathematical statement could tell whether it is true or false? A few years later, Alan Turing made precise the notion of "mechanical procedure" with his definition of a Turing machine, so the question may now be put: Is there a Turing machine which, after reading a mathematical assertion presented to it, eventually writes a (correct) verdict as to whether it is true or not?

If such a machine existed (we shall call it DM, or decision Turing machine), we could use it to solve the halting problem. Here's how. Suppose that we wished to know whether Turing machine T would eventually halt, after being started scanning an input tape with only zeros on it. It can be shown—but the technical details are long and tedious—that we can write a statement H in the formal language of arithmetic which, translated into English, says, "Turing machine T will eventually halt after being started scanning an input tape with only zeros on it." We could then ask the question, "Is H true?" to DM which, sooner or later, would oblige with an answer. At that moment we would know that T will ultimately stop (if DM's answer is yes) or keep running forever (if it is no).

Since the halting problem cannot be solved, DM cannot exist either. In short, there is no mechanical test for truths about the natural numbers—much less for mathematical truths in general. If mathematicians want to discover truth, they must do it the hard way: by proving theorems—they cannot expect a machine to do the job for them.

MECHANICAL LOGIC

One of the things a Turing machine can do is check the validity of certain mathematical proofs. For the purpose of machine-checking, an alleged proof of S, say, must be written as a sequence $E_1, E_2, E_3, \ldots, S$ of formal expressions—the last one being S—such that every expression in the sequence either is an axiom or it can be logically deduced from expressions preceding it. Notice that this is a condensed and formal version of our intuitive idea of a proof, namely, a chain of facts, which are either unquestionably true (the axioms) or logical consequences of previously established facts.

The Proof-Checking Turing machine (let us call it PC) takes as input a sequence $E_1, E_2, E_3, \ldots, S$ and gives as output yes, if the sequence is a proof (of S) and no if it isn't. Writing PC's program is fairly straightforward except for one detail: We must be able to tell the machine, using finitely many instructions, how to recognize an axiom when it sees one. This can be easily accomplished if there is only a finite number of axioms—for example, by giving the machine the complete list, appropriately encoded. But if there are infinitely

81

many of them, then the existence of PC will depend on our ability to pack the information for detecting an axiom into a finite set of instructions.

We also have to instruct PC how to check whether E_i logically follows from some of the expressions $E_1, E_2, E_3, \ldots, E_{i-1}$ preceding it. Fortunately, logicians solved this problem for us long ago by reducing logical inference to the application of a few, very explicit, formal rules. These rules are so "mechanical" that a Turing machine can understand them. And so, by sequentially testing $E_1, E_2, E_3, \ldots$, for axiom or logical consequence, PC can tell us whether or not the input is a proof.

To sum up, a Turing machine can check the logic of a proof all right, but it may have trouble recognizing axioms. When the proofs concern arithmetical propositions, this deficiency will turn out to be an insurmountable obstacle.

The Limits of Formal Reasoning

We are now ready to answer one of David Hilbert's questions: Is arithmetic complete? Or, more explicitly: Is there a set of axioms from which all truths about the natural numbers can be logically deduced? The short answer is no. It was a young Austrian logician who broke the bad news in 1930, barely three years after Hilbert had so confidently raised the question in Bologna. In a paper presented to the Vienna Academy of Sciences, Kurt Gödel made public his result, now known as Gödel's First Incompleteness Theorem: No formal system of axioms is strong enough to prove from them all true arithmetical statements if we require that the notion of proof be itself formal, that is, verifiable by some "mechanical test"—a computer program, for instance. (There is a Second Incompleteness Theorem, dealing with the consistency question.)

Since its publication in 1931, Gödel's result has been the subject of countless technical and popular accounts; articles, essays, and books by the most competent mathematicians and philosophers. Why try again? Because, as Ivar Ekeland wrote in the introduction to his superb *Mathematics and the Unexpected*, "I believe that there is still something to be said, and that the same old story can be told another way."[5]

Let us allow young Gödel himself (he was only twenty-five) to introduce us to his discovery: "The development of mathematics toward greater precision has led, as is well known, to the formalization of large tracts of it, so that one can prove any theorem using nothing but a few mechanical rules. The most comprehensive formal systems that have been set up hitherto are the system of *Principia Mathematica* [due to Alfred Whitehead and Bertrand Russell, in 1925] on the one hand, and the Zermelo-Fraenkel axiom system of set theory [further developed by J. von Neumann] on the other. These two systems are so comprehensive that in them all methods of proof today used in mathematics are formalized, that is, reduced to a few axioms and rules of inference. One might therefore conjecture that these axioms and rules of inference are sufficient to decide *any* mathematical question that can at all be formally expressed in these systems. It will be shown below that this is not the case, that on the contrary there are in the two systems mentioned relatively simple problems in the theory of integers that cannot be decided on the basis of the axioms."[6]

The last sentence means that there are undecidable propositions S that cannot be proved or disproved, that is, neither S nor its negation can be deduced from the axioms—although one of the two is necessarily true. It is in this sense that the axiom systems Gödel refers to are "incomplete"—since not all arithmetical truths can be logically derived from them.

Here are the bare bones of Gödel's argument. Using a clever encoding method later called Gödel numbering, each formal expression can be assigned a natural number. Then, some formal expressions, ostensibly saying something about the natural numbers, can also be interpreted as saying something about other formal expressions. In particular, Gödel shows by an ingenious argument the existence of an expression G that asserts something about itself, roughly equivalent to "I am not formally provable." Now, if G is false, then a false statement—G—would be deducible from the axioms. We must clearly rule out this possibility if our formalization is to be consistent. So, G must be true: an arithmetical truth that cannot be logically deduced from the axioms.

And so, contrary to a widespread belief, truth and deducibility are different things—a conclusion rich in implications for those interested in the philosophy of mathematics. From a formalist's perspective, however, mathematical statements are merely strings of symbols with no interpretation, and therefore they are neither true nor false. The assertion that truth is not the same thing as deducibility then becomes meaningless; for there is no truth, only deducibility.

FROM ONE UNSOLVABLE PROBLEM TO ANOTHER (AND BACK)

In a certain sense, it is the unsolvability of the halting problem that prevents arithmetic from being complete. But we could also put it the other way around and say that the incompleteness of arithmetic is responsible for the halting problem having no solution. In fact, the completeness and the halting questions are equivalent problems. By this we mean that a solution for any one of them could be used to solve the other, so that either both are solvable or none of them is—they sink or swim together.

In showing their interdependence we shall outline an alternative proof of Gödel's theorem. Our argument may be summed up as follows: the completeness of arithmetic would imply the existence of DM (the decision Turing machine); but then, as we have already shown, we could construct another Turing machine that would solve the halting problem—a machine that cannot exist. In just one sentence: if arithmetic were complete, the halting problem could be solved; but since the latter can't, we must conclude that the former isn't.

Suppose that A is a set of axioms from which all arithmetical truths can be derived using the (formal) rules of inference. Here is a recipe to construct DM. To decide whether the statement S in the language of arithmetic is true or false, we feed PC (the Proof-Checking machine), one after the other, all possible finite sequences $E_1, E_2, E_3, \ldots, E_n$ of meaningful expressions. (Surely there is an infinite number of such sequences, but a standard argument shows that they can be systematically generated by a Turing machine.) Remember that PC will answer "yes" if the input sequence is a proof (of the last expression E_n in the sequence), and "no" if it isn't. Now, either S is true or its negation, not-S, is—that much we already knew, of course. Since all truths can be derived from A, there is either a formal proof of S or a formal proof of not-S. Whichever the case, this proof will sooner or later input PC and elicit an output. At that point we will know that S is true—if PC has found a proof of S—or that S is false—if PC has discovered a proof of not-S.

GAMES THAT MACHINES CANNOT PLAY

It is only the very unsophisticated outsider who
imagines that mathematicians make discoveries by
turning the handle of some miraculous machine.
(Godfrey H. Hardy)

There certainly exist sets of axioms from which all arithmetical truths can be derived. For instance, we could take as axioms the set of all true statements. Then all arithmetical truths would be (trivially) provable: a proof of a truth S would simply be S itself. But such complete sets are not recognizable by Turing machines, and so proofs based on them cannot be formalized. In short, no axiomatic system for arithmetic can be both formal and complete. For Aubert Daigneault, a mathematician at the University of Montreal, Gödel proved that when we speak of "natural numbers," we cannot say precisely what we are talking about—that is, we cannot describe the natural numbers by an explicit, "mechanically" verifiable set of axioms.

To truly appreciate the finality of Gödel's blow to Hilbert's episte-mological dream (that of proving all mathematical truths from a single set of axioms) one must comprehend the full import of the Incompleteness Theorem. For the young Austrian logician showed not only the incompleteness of some particular systems, but also that *every* formal system for arithmetic would turn out to be incomplete: there will always be arithmetical truths, expressible in the formal language, which cannot be formally proved. It is therefore impossible to confine number theory—much less all of mathematics—within the framework of a formal system. Mathematicians ought to feel relieved at the news that their science cannot be reduced, even in principle, to a formal game that machines can play.

A COLORING PROBLEM

For all its depth and finality, Gödel's Incompleteness Theorem remains a theoretical result about the limitations of a particular enterprise: the formalization of mathematical proofs. A result, after all, with more philosophical than practical implications. It was for some the end of a dream, reminiscent of another broken dream: the belief of eighteenth-century scientists in the universe as a clock; a transparent and exactly describable universe, predictably ticking away according to Newton's laws.

But the end of a dream often marks the beginning of a better appreciation of reality. Not every mathematical problem may have a solution but the vast majority do,[7] and truth may still be discovered outside the rigidity of a formal system. Mathematics may well be free from contradictions, despite the absence of a consistency proof. And even if a contradiction did turn up, the steel and concrete bridges which were built using mathematical principles will not necessarily fall down, as Stanislaw Ulam once noted. Ulam was a Polish-born mathematician who worked with the top scientists of his time at Los Alamos, during the Second World War.

We have already seen the shortcomings of (even ideal) digital computers for discovering mathematical truth. Computers cannot be programmed to prove all theorems, but as tools for helping mathematicians with certain proofs they are not only valuable but may even be essential.

The mathematical puzzle known as the four-color problem has a long and colorful history.[8] Schoolchildren have for centuries been coloring maps drawn on sheets of paper, using different colors to paint neighboring countries, and probably without ever caring about how many colors they really needed. A quick glance at a map of South America would reveal that Paraguay, Bolivia, Brazil, and Argentina are painted in different colors—as they should, since each country shares a border with the other three. So we need at least four colors. In 1852, Francis Guthrie, a student at London University College, observed that a four-color palette seemed to be enough to color any map. Then he asked whether his conjecture could be proved mathematically (it takes a student to ask a thing like that).

The question appeared to have been settled in 1879 when Alfred Kempe, a barrister, came up with just such a mathematical proof. But eleven years later mathematicians discovered a flaw in his argument. The four-color conjecture was once again an open problem. To make a long story short, let us just say that the problem was finally solved in 1976 by Kenneth Appel and Wolfgang Haken,[9] two mathematicians at the University of Illinois. But theirs was not a traditional paper-and-pencil proof, that is, one that another mathematician could verify. For not only parts of the proof were carried out by a machine, but its correctness cannot be checked without the aid of the computer.

The search for a rigorous proof begins with a translation of the problem into mathematical language. First, we represent each country as a dot; then we join with a line each pair of dots representing neighboring countries. (A clarification is in order here: neighboring countries must share a border that is not just a single point, for otherwise there would be no limit to the number of necessary colors. To see this, think of the countries as the slices of a pie which has been cut up but not yet served. Without the above convention, any two slices would be neighbors [their tips touch] and therefore we would need as many colors as there are slices.) The original map is thus replaced by a certain graph (fig. II.3), and the coloring of countries by the "coloring" of vertices. The requirement that adjacent countries should not share the same color will then be satisfied if vertices joined by an edge are "painted" in different colors.

We shall call a graph five-chromatic if it cannot be painted with fewer than five colors. Guthrie's famous conjecture about map coloring can now be put in the following abstract terms: five-chromatic graphs do not exist. Now, we do not know whether five-chromatic graphs exist, but let us assume they do. Then, there must be one of them, M, say, with the smallest number of vertices—that is, no other five-chromatic graph has fewer vertices than M. To solve the four-color problem it suffices to prove that M cannot exist.

In the first part of their proof, Appel and Haken constructed a list of 1,834 small graphs called configurations and proved, in the traditional sense, that at least one of these must appear as part of any graph. Then their computer program checked that each one of these "unavoidable" configurations possessed a certain property that the minimal five-chromatic graph M cannot possess. Putting together the

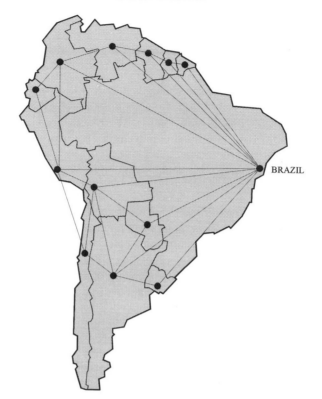

BRAZIL

FIGURE II.3. A map of South America and its graph.
Each country is represented by a dot; two dots are
joined by a line if the corresponding countries share
a border.

mathematicians' argument with the computer's output we get a proof
of Guthrie's conjecture: four colors suffice.

THE COMPUTER'S REVENGE

Appel and Haken's solution was the first famous example of a
computer-assisted proof. These are proofs of some mathematical
proposition which include evidence produced by a computer that
cannot be checked "by hand," the way mathematicians check traditional proofs. In 1989, Herbert Wilf and Doron Zeilberger, both then
at the University of Pennsylvania, wrote a computer program that
proves certain combinatorial identities.[10] These identities are essen-

tially equations asserting that two different ways of counting the objects in a set—one complicated, the other simple—are in fact equal. But Wilf and Zeilberger's proofs do not really depend on the computer because the machine's output can be converted into an ordinary proof. A truly computer-assisted proof, on the other hand, leaves us no choice but to believe the computer. Naturally, such dependence on machines to settle a purely mathematical question— the four-color conjecture—made many people uneasy. Mathematicians are not used to relying on secondhand evidence when it comes to proving theorems.

A few years later, in 1988, another controversial result was announced. A Cray-1A supercomputer had solved a long-standing mathematical problem: Does a projective plane of order 10 exist? A projective plane is made up of "points" and certain sets of points known as "lines." The plane has order n if it contains exactly $n^2 + n + 1$ points and as many lines, and the following four axioms hold: every line is made up of $n + 1$ points; every point lies in $n + 1$ lines; any two (distinct) lines have exactly one point in common; any two (distinct) points lie on exactly one line.

Certain conditions on n guarantee the existence of a projective plane of that order. For example, if $n = p^m$, for some prime number p and exponent $m = 1, 2, 3, \ldots$, there is always a projective plane of order n. Other conditions, if failed to be met by n, imply that there are no planes of order n. It was long known that there are projective planes of every order $n \leq 9$, except $n = 6$. The smallest order n for which the existence or nonexistence of a projective plane remained an open problem was $n = 10$.

What makes the computer particularly suited to hunting for projective planes is the fact that a projective plane can be concretely represented as a binary matrix (this "incidence" matrix has a 1 in the i-th line and j-th column precisely if the j-th point lies on the i-th line). In this way, the search for the hypothetical plane of order 10 becomes a chase for a lattice of 0s and 1s with 111 ($= 10^2 + 10 + 1$) rows and as many columns that satisfies certain conditions. For instance, every row is to contain 11 ones and 100 zeros, to reflect the fact that each line is made up of 11 points; there must also be exactly 11 ones in any given column (since each point must lie in 11 lines).

A quick calculation shows that a straightforward, case-by-case computer inspection of all 111-by-111 binary matrices is to be ruled out because there are far too many of them. Even on a supercomputer capable of performing one trillion (10^{12}) operations per second, the job would take around $10^{3,680}$ years to be completed. The enormity of such a number is hard to grasp. In decimal form, $10^{3,680}$ is written 1 followed by 3,680 zeros, while a generous estimate of the age of the universe is a "mere" 20 billion (2×10^{10}) years, or 2 followed by 10 zeros. Clement Lam, Larry Thiel, and Stanley Swiercz of Concordia University in Montreal managed, by theoretical arguments, to reduce the number of matrices to a more reasonable (but still astronomical) size. They then wrote a series of programs for the computer to take over the search. When the machine completed its calculation without finding a matrix with the required characteristics, the three researchers concluded that no projective plane of order 10 could exist. If there was one, the computer would have found it, summarizes their argument.[11] But a "manual" check of the computer's unsuccessful search was of course out of the question. No wonder such a "proof" left many experts unconvinced and the general public perplexed. Even the *New York Times* joined the debate: "Is a math proof a proof if no one can check it?" asked the title of a December 20, 1988, article on the subject.

The use of computers in proofs introduces an element of uncertainty to which mathematicians, unlike experimental scientists, are not used and may be reluctant to accept. In this context, the computer is in effect an extension of the mathematician's mind, just as the microscope and the radiotelescope are extensions of the physicist's senses. As the above examples seem to suggest, certain propositions may only be proved with the help of this extension, and in such cases the machine becomes an indispensable partner of the mathematician. And so, despite their theoretical limitations, the practical necessity of digital computers in the search for mathematical truth may still be vindicated.

Notes

1. Constance Reid, *Hilbert*, p. 195, Springer-Verlag Berlin-Heidelberg, 1970.

2. Edward Nelson, "Taking Formalism Seriously," *The Mathematical Intelligencer* 15, no. 3 (1993), 8–11.

3. Felix Klein, *Elementary Mathematics from an Advanced Standpoint*, The Macmillan Company, New York, 1932.

4. Reid, *Hilbert*, p. 174.

5. *Mathematics and the Unexpected*, Ivar Ekeland, University of Chicago Press, 1988.

6. Kurt Gödel, "On formally undecidable propositions of *Principia Mathematica* and related systems I" (English translation), in *From Frege to Gödel, a Source Book in Mathematical Logic, 1879–1931*, a collection of original articles edited by Jean Van Heijenoort, Harvard University Press, Cambridge, MA, 1967.

7. Regarding the existence of unsolvable problems, it has been known since Gödel's time that there exist undecidable propositions in ordinary arithmetic. However, most of them are formal constructs, without any mathematical meaning. Since 1931 mathematicians have been looking for a strict mathematical example of an undecidable proposition, one which is mathematically simple and interesting and does not require the numerical coding of notions from logic. The first such examples were only found in 1977. The most striking of them was a reasonably natural theorem of finitary combinatorics, a simple extension of the Finite Ramsey Theorem (see Jeff Paris and Leo Harrington, "A Mathematical Incompleteness in Peano Arithmetic," in *Handbook of Mathematical Logic*, J. Barwise, ed., North-Holland, 1977). In a much more recent paper it is shown that, from a certain topological point of view, the set of propositions that cannot be proved as true within an axiomatic system is the vast majority (C. Calude, H. Juergensen, and M. Zimand, "Is independence an exception?" *Applied Math. Comput.* 66 (1994), 63–76).

8. The rest of this section and the following one are based on the author's article "The burden of proof is on the computer," *New Scientist*, vol. 129, no. 1757, 23 February 1991, pp. 38–40.

9. K. Appel and W. Haken, "Every planar map is four-colorable," *Bull. Amer. Math. Soc.*, vol. 82 (1976), pp. 711–12.

10. Herbert S. Wilf and Doron Zeilberger, "Rational functions certify combinatorial identities," *Journal of the American Mathematical Society*, January 1989.

11. C.W.H. Lam, L. Thiel, and S. Swiercz, "The non-existence of finite projective planes of order 10," *Canadian Journal of Mathematics*, vol. XLI, no. 6, December 1989, pp. 1117–23.

PART THREE
NATURAL SOLUTIONS

*

CHAPTER FIVE

Net Gains

WHAT IS A NEURAL NETWORK?

Soft computing, real-world computing, etc., are
common names for certain forms of natural information
processing that have their original forms in biology.
Fuzzy and probabilistic logic, neural nets, genetic
algorithms, etc., on the other hand, mean alternative
theoretical formalisms by which computing schemes
and algorithms for such tasks can be defined.
(Teuvo Kohonen)[1]

W<small>HEN WE MENTIONED</small> neural networks earlier, we were not referring to the biological arrangements of nerve cells found in living
organisms. These natural networks perform many complex tasks,
from the recognition of sounds and images to memorization and
decision making. The example par excellence is the human brain—although our brain is certainly much more than just a network, or even
a network of networks.

Since biological networks store and process information, they execute a computation of sorts, its most distinctive features being the
massive interconnection of simple computing elements—the neurons
—and the faculty of the network to modify itself by a process similar
to learning. It is this computing ability that the artificial models seek
to capture.

An artificial neural network first appears as a kind of graph, a
convenient notation for certain operations on numerical data. Nodes,
symbolizing the basic computing units, are joined by lines representing the flow of information or data (fig. III.1). From a mathematical
point of view, a given neural network computes a certain mapping or
function f; that is, it associates to "input" data, usually a vector
$(x_1, x_2, \ldots, x_n)$ of numbers, an "output" $f(x_1, x_2, \ldots, x_n)$ which is
also numerical. Thus, the network may be seen as a way of defining

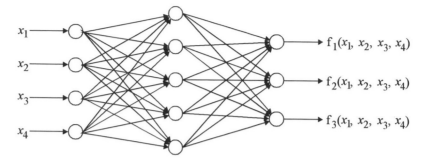

FIGURE III.1. A neural network on paper.

the mapping f when we do not know how to specify it in any other way—or, to paraphrase Marshall McLuhan, the network is the mapping. And so, at the outset, neural networks are mathematical objects. If they are implemented as algorithms on a computer, as electronic circuits or as physical networks consisting of interconnected cells, such systems are also referred to as neural networks. But since these "real" networks are concrete realizations of the ideal ones, the latter are the proper object of investigation.

The inspiration of artificial neural networks may come from nature, but their performance is still far from approaching that of the real thing. Nevertheless, the artificial models have provided an alternative to classical computing methods for solving certain types of problems, especially in cases when an exact solution procedure is unknown or impossible to encode as a program. A typical example of such problems is the classification of patterns. This includes the recognition of sounds and images, but since a "pattern" is a very general concept, many other situations also fall into this category. A computer file may be seen as a pattern, and the classification may consist in deciding whether the file is "clean" or it has been attacked by a computer virus. Once the neural network has been "trained" (as explained later) to recognize the infested files among those in a training set, it can then be expected to detect new contaminated files presented to it. This feat would have been achieved without us having had to specify precisely what a computer virus is. Such an approach is not unlike the training of dogs to detect concealed drugs. The dog eventually learns to recognize a scent as "drug" without ever being provided with an exact definition. This faculty to learn by examples is also present in neural networks when they are used as classifiers.

Just as there are many sorts of automobiles or clocks, there also exist many different kinds of neural networks. Any attempt to classify them begins with some arbitrary choices. Of the many possibilities, we have chosen to distinguish between feedforward, or ordinary, networks and feedback networks. The former act on a given input and, after performing a series of operations, produce an output; in the latter, neuron responses are connected—fed back—to the network. Feedback networks are best described as dynamical systems, in terms of "states" and "transitions." For a given input, the network goes through a sequence of states, in either discrete or continuous time transitions. When—and if—the network reaches some stable state, this final configuration is considered to be the network's response. In what follows, we will mostly analyze the feedforward kind and relegate feedback networks to a separate section.

Both types of networks are composed of interconnected computing units called (artificial) neurons which imitate the behavior of biological neurons—or at least pretend to do so. The first attempt to give a formal definition of a synthetic neuron goes back to 1943. In their famous paper "A logical calculus of the ideas immanent in nervous activities"[2] (much quoted and often misquoted, with "immanent" replaced by the more familiar "imminent"), W. S. McCulloch and W. Pitts gave an elegant mathematical definition of a neuron with multiple binary inputs and a single binary output. Organized into networks, these basic elements could compute simple logical (i.e., Boolean) functions.

More than a decade later, F. Rosenblatt introduced the perceptron,[3] a precursor of many of the present neural network models. Rosenblatt's main motivation for developing the perceptron was to provide a model for certain functions of biological systems. In particular, the way in which such systems store and retrieve information, and how the stored information influences recognition and behavior. He was convinced that (real) neural networks, with their myriad of random interconnections, could not be properly represented by symbolic logic and Boolean algebra. His is therefore a probabilistic model, aimed at providing a mathematical analysis of the overall organization of the nerve net. Rosenblatt was well aware, though, that his model represented only extreme simplifications of the central nervous system.

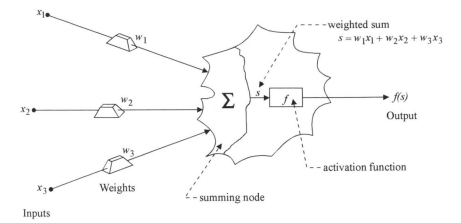

FIGURE III.2. The artificial neuron model.

FROM THE BIOLOGICAL TO THE ARTIFICIAL NEURON

There are two kinds of artificial neurons from which most networks are built. The two models differ mainly in the type of data they can handle, which may be either binary or continuous. In the first case, several binary numbers—x_1, x_2 and x_3, say—enter the artificial neuron as inputs (see fig. III.2). Using the biological nerve cell as a guide, these numbers may be interpreted as the signals sent to the neuron from other neurons. After a short interval, the biological neuron will respond to the aggregation of its inputs by firing a neural pulse. In our mathematical model, the aggregation of inputs is represented by the weighted sum

$$s = w_1 x_1 + w_2 x_2 + w_3 x_3$$

where the "weights" w_1, w_2, and w_3, which can be any real numbers, measure the strength of the connection of each input to the neuron body. These numbers are also known as synaptic weights—from synapse, the name of the contact organ in the biological case.

For the firing of the biological neuron to take place, the combined inputs must exceed a certain threshold value. In the artificial neuron, a typical threshold value is zero, and so it "fires," that is, it produces the output value $f(s) = 1$, if s is greater than zero; otherwise, it does

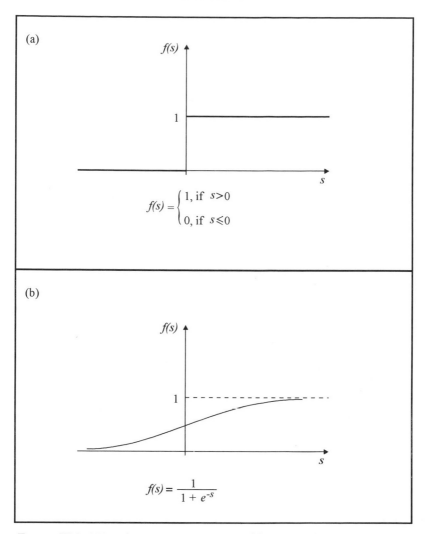

FIGURE III.3. Neural activation functions. (*a*) Binary; (*b*) Continuous.

not fire ($f(s) = 0$). The function f is called the neuron's activation function (fig. III.3 (*a*)).

A continuous neuron accepts any real numbers as inputs and it can respond with any number between 0 and 1 as output—a continuous range of values, or graded response. The activation $f(s)$ of the continuous neuron is also a function of the weighted sum s. Its graph (fig. III.3 (*b*)) is a kind of smoothed-out version of the graph of fig.

III.3 (*a*). One popular choice for f is

$$f(s) = \frac{1}{1 + e^{-s}}$$

known as the sigmoid, but essentially any continuous, monotonically increasing function that takes values between 0 and 1 may serve as an activation function.

To sum up, both the binary and the continuous neuron compute the function $y = f(w_1 x_1 + w_2 x_2 + \cdots + w_n x_n)$ for input $(x_1, x_2, \ldots, x_n)$, a rather modest accomplishment after all. But then consider a single nerve cell in isolation—not very impressive either. Would you have imagined what can be achieved when millions of these primitive cells are interconnected? Likewise, the elementary artificial neuron by itself may not amount to much. It is only when many of these basic computing units are put together that totally unexpected and potentially useful new properties may develop. This point was well made by John Hopfield, a pioneer of neural computation, in his 1982 seminal paper[4] (to which we shall return later): "Much of the architecture of regions of the brains of higher animals must be made from a proliferation of simple local circuits with well-defined functions. The bridge between simple circuits and the complex computational properties of higher nervous systems may be the spontaneous emergence of new computational capabilities from the collective behavior of large numbers of simple processing elements."

NETWORKS AS OPEN ALGORITHMS

If we want to solve a problem on a digital computer we must provide it with a solution strategy in the form of precise instructions—a program. One of the distinctive features of neural computation is the absence of such a fixed set of commands. A neural network may rather be viewed as an incomplete program, or "open" algorithm, in the sense that certain numerical parameters—the weights—are not specified by the programmer. The weights are calculated during a "training phase," a gradual procedure that requires some data (the training set) and another program (the learning algorithm). During the training phase the network "learns" to respond in a certain way to the data presented to it. Terms such as "training" and "learning" may suggest that a process similar to animal or human learning takes place, but they are merely convenient (if not misleading) analogies. What neural network practitioners call "learning" is in fact "calculation," and it is as removed from actual human learning as is a mathematical neuron from a biological one.

The reason why the weights cannot be specified up front is simply that one has normally no clue as to the relation from cause to effect, that is, how different weight values affect the computation of the network. This state of affairs results from the very essence of neural networks, which are basically "black boxes" whose behavior is largely unpredictable. The user can select the network "architecture"—the number and type of neurons, the way they are interconnected, and so on—but weights cannot in general be rationally set or even guessed, they can only be "learned" (a notable exception is the Hopfield feedback net—the subject of an upcoming section—whose weights are set up front).

There are disadvantages to this black-box approach to problem solving, for it is nearly impossible to use our intuition the way we do when writing or modifying a computer program—in order to fix a bug, for instance. The obvious advantage, on the other hand, is that the network can be made to perform tasks we would not know how to spell out in an explicit, algorithmic form.

Boiled down to the essentials, a neural network maps input data to output data, and in this respect it is a computing device. Both the input and the output data are typically finite strings $[x_1, x_2, \ldots, x_n]$ of numbers called n-dimensional vectors. The numbers x_i may range over a certain interval, for instance $-1 \leq x_i \leq 1$, in which case we speak of continuous data, or they may take on only two values, such as 0 and 1 (binary data). The type of data used depends on the purpose of the computation, which brings us to the practical question of what can actually be achieved with a neural network.

PATTERN RECOGNIZERS

Neural networks are very good at pattern recognition and classification tasks. A pattern is a very general concept that includes images, sounds, and forms such as printed characters (letters, numerals, or punctuation marks). To be specific, let us assume that there are 95 characters. Each of these may be physically represented as a rectangular grid called a pixel grid. If a 7 × 10 grid is used, then each of its 70 positions may be either black or white (fig. III.4). This affords an astronomical number of possible dot configurations, but we need only 95 of them to represent our printed characters. For the purpose of network processing, a character is encoded as a string of 70 bits—a binary vector. A 1 (respectively a 0) in a given position meaning that the corresponding dot in the pixel grid is black (white). The neural network then has 70 input neurons, one for each bit (or pixel) position and 95 output neurons, corresponding to the 95 "classes" of characters. (This is a rather special situation; in most classification problems a class will be composed of more than just one pattern.) The remaining neurons in the network, the so-called "hidden" neurons, are used for computation purposes only.

When a character, encoded as a 70-dimensional binary vector, is presented to the neural network, the latter will respond by setting to 1 exactly one of its 95 output neurons, thus signaling the result of the classification. In this way the network associates—correctly or incorrectly—each printed character with a "class." During the training phase, the neural network "learns" the correct associations in much the same way an infant recognizes flash cards (it's a dog, it's a cat, etc.) under the supervision of a teacher. The 95 characters (the training set) are fed to the network one at a time. The network responds by returning a class number for each one of them. Whenever a character is misclassified, the learning algorithm will adjust the weights in such a way as to increase the likelihood of a correct classification the next time around (this involves the clever use of

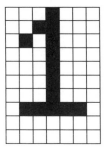 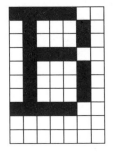

FIGURE III.4. Pixel grids. Dot-matrix printer characters (7-column by 10-row) as defined by Apple Computer in 1986.

102

mathematical techniques, as will be explained in later sections). The training cycle continues until the network correctly recognizes all characters. This may require presenting the training set to the network hundreds, if not thousands, of times. The values of the weights at the end of the training phase are adopted as final, and the network will then be ready for operation.

Notice that at the most abstract level there are no pixels, characters, or classes involved here. The network merely computes a function; that is, to each 70-dimensional binary vector (the input), it associates a particular 95-dimensional binary vector (the output). It is our interpretation that gives the computation its meaning. Thus, *we* see, or interpret, each input as a black or white pixel and the input vector (i.e., all the 70 pixels considered in a given order) as a printed character. Similarly, the output neuron that is "turned on" (with value 1), indicates to us which input character the network has—accurately or not—recognized. Finally, it is we who view this particular computation as a classification process.

In the above example (which is based on an actual application[5]), the network eventually learns to classify every input pattern correctly. This is perhaps not surprising, given that the members of each class can be exactly defined as certain configurations of dots. In a more typical situation there will be patterns whose class might be very difficult—or impossible—to determine, even for a human classifier. Such is the case when the patterns are the handwritten numerals that appear on zip codes. Even if these numerals can somehow be represented as pixel grids, it is impossible to tell precisely which dot configurations correspond to the different ways people write the numeral "5," for instance. Under those circumstances, no neural network—or any other classifier, for that matter—can be expected to perform the classification with a success rate of 100 percent. Fortunately, another useful feature of neural computation comes into play here: the ability of a neural network to "generalize." This roughly means that if a neural network has learned to classify a large number of sample patterns that are in some sense typical, it can then be expected to correctly classify new, unknown patterns—at least most of the time.

Our next example involves a task that baffles even human experts: after examining a computer program, decide whether or not it has been infected by a computer virus.

OF VIRUSES AND MEN

The metaphor is one of the scientific writer's best friends. When used wisely, it can serve to enhance the understanding of a difficult concept and to make in the reader's mind an impression he or she will not soon forget. But the writer's friend may easily turn into an insidious enemy. Metaphors will cause more harm than good if they are ill-chosen, abused, or stretched too far by the author—or mistaken for the real thing by the reader.

On the topic of a particular type of computer malfunction, the distinction between metaphor and reality is usually blurred in the extreme—for better or worse. When tragedy strikes, a hard-drive or computer memory are no longer inanimate objects but become living organisms that have been "infected" by a "virus." A similarly "infected" diskette may spread the "pathogen agent" around, causing hitherto "healthy" software to "catch the disease." The "viral attack," which may reach "epidemic" proportions, can be stopped only after the virus has been "isolated" and "dissected" for study, and a "cure" for it finally found. The so-called Jerusalem virus, which appeared in Israel at the end of 1987, was referred to in the press as a "killer" virus.

A computer virus (a term coined by Adleman in the early 1980s[6]) is in fact a section of a program that contains instructions for self-replication, and capable of attaching copies of itself to other programs or regions of a disk. The famous Jerusalem virus first copies itself to memory when a program where it "lives" is executed, and from there it infects any program later executed by the host system. These infected programs can themselves propagate in the same fashion, eventually contaminating other computer systems. The unpleasant consequences of a viral attack may range from a scrolling screen to the loss of the entire contents of a hard disk, resulting in the temporary—or, if nothing is done, permanent—crippling of the victim's system.

It is true that the similarities between a biological virus and its electronic counterpart are striking. Both attach themselves to an individual (organism or computer) and, in the process of replicating themselves, play havoc with some vital functions of their hosts: destruction of cells, or even life, in the one case; loss of data, programs, and the ability to operate properly, in the other. While most viruses are specific to some population (monkeys or DOS files), others might have the ability to jump species (from monkey to human—as was the case with the AIDS virus—or from DOS to Macintosh software). The most damaging computer viruses are (fortunately) the least likely to spread, just as deadly strains of viruses are rare while relatively innocuous ones—the common cold virus, for instance—are widespread. Another common feature is the indiscriminate nature of their attacks: once unleashed, both biological and electronic viruses strike at any potential victim that gets in their way.

The analogy comes apart on the motivation behind such a destructive behavior. For all their devastating effects, biological viruses cannot be accused of being intrinsically evil. Computer viruses, on the other hand, are consciously created and disseminated by some human who is well aware of their wicked design.

The Virus Hunters

Scattered all over the world, from California to Iceland, a small army of dedicated men and women works around the clock to counteract the effects of a human-made electronic plague. They are the virus fighters, an informal, international community united in their struggle to detect and remove computer viruses. This is done mostly through the use of traditional methods, which rely upon analysis of each new virus by human experts. But a few years from now, this case-by-case approach will be too slow to cope with new viruses spreading rapidly through global networks such as the Internet. Then, a much faster, automatic, and generic response to an outbreak will be required.

In their search for the virus-protection techniques of the future, a team at the High Integrity Computing Laboratory of IBM's Thomas J. Watson Research Center turned to nature for inspiration. Since computer viruses resemble real ones in many ways, the experts looked for clues in the defense mechanisms that living organisms have evolved against disease. Using this "biological" approach, the team headed by Steve White and Jeffrey Kephart developed a virus detector based on a neural network. The technique was later incorporated into a commercial product—IBM's AntiVirus software.

In order to get back to normal, infected computers need specialized assistance just as very sick humans do. A virus-fighting expert must first disassemble the virus code to discover how it works and precisely what it does. The expert then selects a "signature," or short sequence of code (from 16 to 32 bytes long), representing a portion of the virus operations (instructions for self-replication or some other suspicious activity, for example) that are characteristic of the intruder but unlikely to be found in an ordinary computer program. This information can then be encoded into virus scanners—programs that search files, memory, and other locations for the presence of viruses.

The detection of a virus in a system is normally followed by a disinfection process to restore infected programs to their original state. A serious drawback of scanning and repair mechanisms is that they can be applied only to known viruses, or variants of them. Present scanners and disinfectors therefore require frequent updates, as new viruses are discovered. Once detected, each individual virus strain must be analyzed in order to extract the information that will neutralize it, an operation that may take several days.

The IBM team recognizes that the idea of using biological analogies to defend computers from viruses is not new (W. H. Murray proposed a similar approach in 1988[7]), but they claim to be the first ones to have taken the analogy seriously, to the point of having actually created antivirus technology that is inspired by biology.[8]

Artificial Neurons vs. Artificial Viruses

The problem of deciding whether any given computer program is viral or not is algorithmically unsolvable. In simpler terms, the perfect virus detector cannot be built. The reasons for this negative result are not merely practical but more fundamental: a universal virus detector program could be used to decide whether an arbitrary Turing machine will eventually terminate its computation. But, as we have seen in chapter 3, no algorithm can solve this halting problem,[9] so no universal virus detector can exist either. Of course, it is always possible to devise efficient, if less sweeping, virus catchers that work well in practice.

The detection of computer viruses may be viewed as a problem in pattern classification with only two possible classes: "infected" and "noninfected." A simpler but important subproblem is the classification of boot sector viruses, which account for about 80 percent of the most common viruses. To "boot" a computer is to "instruct itself to get going" or "to pick itself up by its bootstraps." A boot sector is a small sequence of code (512 bytes long in IBM-compatible PCs) that tells the computer how to do precisely that.

Guided by both practical and theoretical considerations, the IBM team extracted about fifty 3-byte strings, called features, that appear frequently in viral boot sectors but infrequently in legitimate ones. Given an arbitrary 512-byte boot sector, the presence (1) or absence (0) of each feature defines a binary vector. This vector becomes the input to a single-layer network with a continuous activation function. The network weights were computed by back-propagation (see next section) using some 100 training samples, of which about three-quarters were viral. A network output value greater than zero would indicate the presence of a virus; otherwise the boot sector would be declared healthy.

Since in this case there are only two classes, "infected" and "healthy," two types of classification errors are possible: false-positives (a healthy file erroneously declared infected) and false-negatives (a contaminated file slipping through undetected). For this particular application, avoiding false positives is crucial. Frequent false alarms on thousands of computers would leave users worse-off than they would have been without virus protection.

Test runs of the system resulted in a false-negative rate of 10 to 15 percent and a false positive rate of 0.02 percent. Commenting on this performance, the team predicted that 85 percent of new boot sector viruses will be detected, with a tiny chance of false positives on legitimate boot sectors. The neural network classifier has in fact already caught several new viruses, displaying one of antivirus software's most desirable qualities: the ability to deal with new viruses on its own.

SEARCHING FOR THE IDEAL WEIGHTS

The example we give below, although extremely simple, illustrates well how geometric intuition coupled with the efficiency of linear algebra may be used to "train" a neural network. By "training" we understand finding a set of weights which would result in the network performing a specific task. In the present case we would like the network—actually a single neuron—to separate the sheep from

107

the goat, or, in specialist's jargon, to classify the elements of a given set into two disjoint classes.

Suppose that we have five numbers, $x_1, x_2, \ldots, x_5$, divided into two classes: x_1 and x_5 are in class A_0 and the rest in class A_1. We wish to teach an artificial neuron to classify these numbers correctly, that is, to respond by 0 or 1 depending on the class containing the number x_i presented to it. For technical reasons, we encode the numbers as 2-dimensional vectors $y_i = [x_i, 1]$, whose second coordinate is always 1. Consequently, our neuron will have two inputs, one for each coordinate, and one output to give its answer. Training the neuron then amounts to finding the weights w_1 and w_2 that induce the correct classification. In other words, the neuron must "learn" to compute the function

$$f(w_1 x_i + w_2) = \begin{array}{l} 0, \text{ if } x_i \text{ is in } A_0 \\[1em] 1, \text{ if } x_i \text{ is in } A_1. \end{array}$$

If we use a neuron with the activation function pictured in figure III.3 (a)—that is, $f(s) = 1$ or 0, according to whether s is positive or not—then our problem may be stated as follows:

Find w_1 and w_2 such that

$$w_1 x_i + w_2 < 0, \text{ for } i = 1 \text{ or } 5;$$
$$\text{and} \tag{1}$$
$$w_1 x_i + w_2 > 0, \text{ for } i = 2, 3, \text{ or } 4.$$

It is not hard to see that there are many—in fact infinitely many—possible solutions for w_1 and w_2, and that these solutions may be computed by mathematical reasoning alone; that is, we could bypass the training procedure altogether. However, in more complex situations training might be the most efficient—if not the only—way to determine the appropriate weights.

The possible weights may be seen here as the coordinates of weight vectors $W = [w_1, w_2]$. These vectors are graphically represented as points in the 2-dimensional space E^2 (the coordinate plane) or, alternatively, as directed segments, the way vectors are pictured in linear algebra textbooks. By a simple geometrical argument it can be shown that the weight vectors W satisfying the above condition (1) of correct classification all lie in a region S of E^2 that is the intersection of five half-planes.

The training algorithm begins with an initial weight vector $W_1 = [w_{11}, w_{12}]$ that may be arbitrarily chosen (any vector except $[0, 0]$ would do). Using the five given numbers and their respective classes as data, the algorithm must lead us from W_1 to some W_n in S by a succession of computation steps—ideally, in the most direct way. Presented with the first number x_1 (encoded as $[x_1, 1]$), the algorithm simulates the computation of the neuron by calculating $f(w_{11} x_1 + w_{12})$ and thus responds with a 0 or a 1. If this answer correctly classifies x_1, then no weight adjustment needs to take place. But if the classification is incorrect, the current weight vector W_1 is replaced by a new one, W_2, so as to increase the likelihood of a correct classification the next time x_1 will be examined by the neuron (the calculation of W_2 is explained below). The procedure is then repeated using as input each of the other numbers $x_2, \ldots, x_5$, and starting all over again with $x_1, x_2, \ldots$ until a weight vector W_n which correctly classifies all five numbers is obtained. By a mathematical argument, it can be shown that the following rule for weight adjustment will produce such a W_n in a finite number of steps.

Weight adjustment rule:

Suppose that x_i has been incorrectly classified using the weight vector $W_k = [w_1, w_2]$. Then, the new weight vector should be

$$W_{k+1} = [w_1 \pm x_i, w_2 \pm 1],$$

that is, W_{k+1} is obtained by adding or subtracting the vector y_i to W_k. The plus sign applies when the misclassified number x_i is in class A_1 and the minus sign when it is in class A_0.

Figure III.5 illustrates the geometry behind the adjustment rule. If, say, $x_2 = 3$—which is encoded as the vector $y_2 = [3, 1]$—then $3w_1 + w_2 = 0$ is the equation of a straight line L perpendicular to y_2. This line divides the coordinate plane into the two half-planes H_0 and H_1, whose equations are:

$$3w_1 + w_2 < 0 \ (H_0) \text{ and } 3w_1 + w_2 > 0 \ (H_1).$$

Since x_2 belongs to the class A_1, its correct classification requires that $3w_1 + w_2 > 0$ (for the neuron's output to be 1). Therefore, any weight vector $[w_1, w_2]$ in H_1 will effect the proper classification,

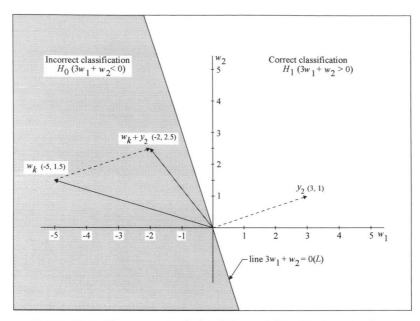

FIGURE III.5. The geometry behind the weight-adjustment rule.

while all weight vectors in H_0 will result in a classification error. Suppose that the current weight vector is $W_k = [-5, 1.5]$. Now, $3(-5) + 1.5 = -13.5 < 0$, so W_k is in H_0 and we have a misclassification. To rectify this mistake, we must move W_k over to H_1. The shortest path toward H_1 is in the direction of the perpendicular to L, and this is precisely the direction of $y_2 = [3, 1]$. By adding y_2 to W_k, we move the weight vector toward H_1—and in the most efficient way. Should we encounter the other kind of misclassification (i.e., the current weight vector is in H_1, while the correct weights are those in H_0) then subtracting y_2 would move W_k in the opposite direction, since y_2 always points toward the "positive" half-plane (H_1).

In a more general (and realistic) situation the inputs will be n-dimensional vectors $(x_1, x_2, \ldots, x_n)$ or "patterns" (the inputs of a network are usually called patterns, regardless of their particular nature) and the trained neuron will be expected to do more than just classify the patterns in the training set: it should also be able to class correctly new, unknown patterns presented to it, at least most of the time. For this to happen, certain conditions on the distribution of the patterns must be satisfied—for example, the set of all patterns should be roughly disposed in clusters around the "sample" patterns used for training.

Performing more sophisticated tasks would require the combined power of many interconnected neurons. These are usually arranged in layers, in such a way that the outputs from the neurons in one layer become the inputs to the neurons in the next one. Their learning algorithms are consequently much more sophisticated than the simple one just presented.

The mathematical framework for the training of layered networks was laid down by the American mathematician Paul Werbos in his 1974 doctoral dissertation.[10] One of the most popular—and most effective—training methods is the so-called error back-propagation algorithm (discussed in Appendix 4), which systematically modifies the weights so that the output of the network increasingly approaches the desired response.

Most learning algorithms have basically the same format: A set of patterns—the training set—is submitted to the network many times in succession. If the response of the network to a given pattern is incorrect, the algorithm adjusts the weights so that a certain "error" is reduced. Because the correct answers are known and they are used to gradually improve the network's performance, this type of training is called supervised learning. The comparison between desired and actual responses—and the weight adjustments, when necessary—continue until all patterns in the training set have been "learned" with an acceptable overall error. This global error is usually computed by adding the individual errors over the entire training set (it is unrealistic to expect a perfect response record, that is, an error equal to zero). The whole process boils down to trying to solve an optimization problem: that of minimizing the global error, which is usually a hopelessly complex function of a large number of variables.

THE IMPORTANCE OF BEING NUMEROUS

Computational properties, of use to biological
organisms or to the construction of computers, can
emerge as collective properties of systems having a
large number of simple equivalent components.
(John J. Hopfield)[11]

111

During the 1970s, the limitations of simple networks based on Rosenblatt's perceptrons had led to a decline of the initial enthusiasm for neural models. But in 1982, after a lull of a decade or so, interest in neural networks was rekindled following the publication of a paper by a distinguished physicist. In a seminal article,[12] John J. Hopfield brought together a number of ideas, most of which were perhaps not totally new, with a clear and powerful mathematical analysis. We already knew that computations produce numbers. Hopfield argued that number could spontaneously generate computation or, more exactly, that "computation" can emerge as a collective property of systems having a large number of simple components that interact with each other.

According to Hopfield, thanks to our understanding of basic electronic circuits we can plan the complex circuits that are essential to large computers. "Because evolution has no such plan," he wrote, "it becomes relevant to ask whether the ability of large collections of neurons to perform 'computational' tasks may in part be a spontaneous collective consequence of having a large number of interacting simple neurons." He then proposed a mathematical model—afterwards known as a Hopfield net—in which computational properties arise due to the interaction of many elementary cells rather than to circuitry. The collective properties of the model produce a "content-addressable" memory that can restore missing information.

Consider the reference "T. Denoeux and R. Lengelle, 'Initializing Back-Propagation Networks with Prototypes,' Neural Networks 6, no. 3, pp. 351–63 (1993)." This information may be "corrupted" and become, say, "Denueux and Lenjel, Neural Networks (1993)." A content-addressable memory should then be capable of retrieving the complete reference on the basis of the corrupted data. From a dynamical system point of view, information that is incomplete or contains errors may be seen as an unstable point in a state space, while the correct entry would correspond to a stable point (or attractor). The complete, original information might be retrieved by forcing the state of the system (the information being processed) to flow toward a stable point from anywhere within regions around it.

Hopfield observed that if the dynamics of a physical system is dominated by a substantial number of stable states to which it is attracted, we can then regard the system as a content-addressable memory. He conjectured that the stability of memories may spontaneously arise in systems made up of a large number of simple interacting elements. If, in addition, we can choose any set of states and readily force them to be the stable states, then the system becomes a potentially useful memory device.

NET DYNAMICS

A Hopfield net can be used to retrieve patterns, such as black-and-white images, that might contain errors or have suffered loss of information. The original patterns are called prototypes. We shall give a simple example of a Hopfield net in which the prototypes are the ten digits $0, 1, 2, \ldots, 9$.

Using a 10×12 dot-matrix representation, each digit can be described by a binary word, that is, by a vector of 120 binary numbers: $+1$, to represent a black dot, and -1, a white one. By an appropriate choice of connection weights (as explained below), these prototypes can be "stored" in the net's "memory." During its operation phase (or recall), the network will try to associate a given input pattern (i.e., a 120-dimensional binary vector) with a prototype—ideally, the one that most closely matches the input. Unlike the weights of the networks we have discussed so far, those of a Hopfield net are not "learned" but set by the user up front. As we mentioned above, setting the weights may be seen as storing the prototype patterns in the network's memory. Here is the basic idea guiding the choice of the weights.

Suppose that in each of the 10 prototypes the 15th and the 78th bits are identical, that is, they are either both $+1$ or both -1. In trying to restore a partially corrupted input pattern C, the network will gradually modify C in order to bring it in line with one of the prototypes (P, say). If C is to converge toward P, neuron 15 should strongly urge neuron 78 to match its current state, since in P these two bits must be the same. If the bits at the two positions happen to agree only in 8 prototypes, then neuron 15 should send neuron 78 a somewhat weaker signal to copy its state. In general, the bits at positions i and j will agree in some prototypes and disagree in others. The measure of signal strength will be the difference between agreements and disagreements. For instance, if the i-th and j-th bits agree in 8 prototype patterns and disagree in the other 2, then w_{ij} will be set at $8 - 2 = 6$; if they agree (disagree) in all 10 prototypes,

113

then $w_{ij} = 10 - 0 = 10$ ($w_{ij} = 0 - 10 = -10$); if they agree in exactly half of the prototypes, then $w_{ij} = 5 - 5 = 0$.

Denoting by P_i the i-th bit of prototype pattern P, the product $P_i P_j$ will be equal to 1 if bits i and j of P are identical, and it will be equal to -1 if they are different. Then, the strength of the connection from neuron j to neuron i is captured by the following formula:

$$w_{ij} = \sum P_i P_j \tag{2}$$

where the summation ranges over all the prototypes P. (The formula adds 1 if the i-th and j-th bits of a prototype are the same, and it subtracts 1 if they are different.) Weights w_{ii} are set equal to zero, that is, no connection is allowed from a neuron back to itself.

What happens during the operation of the network? At time $t = 0$, an input pattern C (a 120-dimensional binary vector) is imposed on the network. The i-th bit of C becomes the initial state of neuron i, so that, at time zero, the network merely records the input pattern C. At subsequent time steps, $t = 1, 2, 3, \ldots$, the neurons will undergo state changes which correspond to gradual modifications (one bit at a time) of the original input pattern C.

It is important to emphasize that only one neuron per time step is allowed to "fire," that is, to look at its input and (possibly) change its state. Which neuron is allowed to fire is determined randomly, with the average firing rate being the same for all neurons. This "asynchronous" updating mode intends to model the random propagation delays of nerve signals found in biological systems.

The state of the firing neuron—the i-th neuron, say—at time $t + 1$ is decided on the information it receives from all the other neurons at time t. For example, if w_{ij} is -8 and j is in state $+1$, then the input signal coming to i from j will be the product $(-8)(+1) = -8$. Similar signals, $+4$, 0, $+10$, -2, and so forth, arriving from the other neurons may be interpreted as "votes" on the decision the i-th neuron should make regarding its next state: positive votes urge i to fire (i.e., to assume state $+1$) while negative ones favor the nonfiring state -1. The neuron's own state does not influence its decision, since there is no feedback from a neuron to itself. Neuron i will then fire (state $+1$) if the sum of the votes is positive, otherwise it will not fire (state -1).

To sum up, here is the formula used by the i-th neuron to compute its next state:

$$\mu_i(t+1) = f\left[\sum_{j=1} w_{ij}\mu_j(t)\right]$$

where $\mu_j(t)$ denotes the state of neuron j at time t and f is the threshold (activation) function:

$f(s) = +1$, if s is greater than 0; $f(s) = -1$, otherwise.

The vector $\mu(t) = (\mu_1(t), \mu_2(t), \ldots, \mu_n(t))$ represents the state of a network of n neurons at time t. It is convenient to visualize the possible states of the network as vertices of a "hypercube" in a space of n dimensions. For $n = 3$, the eight 3-dimensional vectors with components $+1$ or -1 are the vertices of an ordinary cube. For n greater than 3, it is no longer possible to draw the hypercube, but we can still imagine it. As time changes from t to $t + 1$, the state of the network travels from one vertex to an adjacent one (since a single neuron is allowed to fire at time t, only one coordinate of the state vector can change at any given time step). The network is considered to have converged when (and if) this journey from vertex to vertex ceases, that is, when the network's state becomes stable.

The equilibrium state S represents the network's response or restored memory, which is generally the prototype that most closely resembles the input pattern. Given its nondeterministic nature, the network may converge to a spurious pattern—one not present in the prototype set—or exhibit a chaotic behavior and keep wandering in a small region of the state space.

In one of Hopfield's computer simulations, m patterns (for various values of m) were randomly generated and stored according to equation (2). Each of these m "prototypes" was then used as input and the network was allowed to evolve until it became stable. Hopfield's rationale for choosing random prototypes was that the information preprocessed by a nervous system for efficient storage would appear random, and he cited as an example the random character of sequences of DNA. "The random memory vectors thus simulate efficiently encoded real information, as well as representing our ignorance."[13]

115

Results of the simulations suggested that the number of prototypes should be small compared to the number of neurons, or else error in recall might be severe. Hopfield concluded—and experience confirmed—that, for reasonably accurate recall, a rate of 15 prototypes per 100 neurons should not be exceeded. Thus, recalling 10 prototypes would necessitate about 70 neurons and close to 5,000 weights.

When the neurons are allowed to have continuous activation functions (fig. III.3 (*b*)), state changes of the network no longer occur at discrete time steps but take place continuously. Such systems generally possess a rather complex dynamics, and the analysis of their behavior requires sophisticated mathematical tools.

The initial enthusiasm generated by Hopfield's work in the mid-1980s was followed by more sober expectations. Even if as early as 1987 AT & T Bell Laboratories had announced the development of neural chips largely based on the Hopfield network,[14] the applications of Hopfield's model remain limited. In 1992, Jacek M. Zurada, an active researcher in the field, assessed the situation in these terms: "The solutions offered by the networks are hard to track back or to explain and are often due to random factors. [. . .] However, it should be stressed that the dynamical systems approach to cognitive tasks is still in an early development stage. The application of the dynamical models to real-size optimization or association problems beyond their present scope will require a great deal of further scientific development."[15] In short, the technique might be promising but don't get too excited too soon.

Developing a Taste for Real Raspberries

Anyone can recognize a fresh raspberry, but it is quite a different matter to tell whether a sample of fruit pulp is 100 percent raspberry, especially if it is frozen or in sulphited form. This is a problem commercial manufacturers of fruit preserves must face when they use fruit pulps to prepare those delicious, homemade-style jams and marmalades. How to be sure that the supplier has not added some sugar or cheaper fruits to the raspberry, to stretch the pulp as well as the profit margin?

A novel method for detecting adulteration of raspberry pulps, based on spectroscopic techniques and the Fourier transform (a powerful mathematical tool), was developed by a team of researchers at the Institute of Food Research in Norwich, UK. The method identifies samples using sections of the mid-infrared spectrum, a kind of molecular "fingerprint" highly sensitive to the precise chemical composition of the sample.[16] But since different fruit pulps may have very similar spectra, changes occurring in the spectrum due to the adulteration with another fruit might not always be obvious to the eye. J. K. Holland, E. K. Kemsley, and R. H. Wilson, three IFR researchers, decided to train a neural network to help them distinguish between the spectra of pure raspberry and that of other (cheaper) pulps, especially adulterated raspberry.

They began by collecting a database of some 900 mid-infrared spectra of different types of fruit pulp as well as raspberry pulps that had been mixed with sucrose, apple, or plum, all potential adulterant materials. The database was then separated into three roughly equal groups: a training set for developing the network model; a tuning set for adjusting the model's parameters, and a test set to validate the performance of the network. About two-thirds of the samples in each set came from fruits other than raspberry; the remaining third was equally divided between pure and adulterated raspberry spectra. For the purpose of data analysis, each spectrum is represented by 50 so-called principal component scores.

The network has a first layer of 8 neurons, each of which receives as input the 50 principal component scores of a sample. The outputs from this input layer are then passed on to a single neuron that produces as final output a number between 0 and 1. In order to obtain the desired network response—1 for raspberry, and 0 for non-raspberry—the values of the 408 synaptic weights were adjusted by back-propagation. At the end of each training cycle, the tuning set was used to compute the prediction errors (the difference between the desired value and the network's output). When the sum of the squared errors over the entire tuning set reached a minimum—more precisely, when it increased for 10 successive cycles—the learning was terminated. This kind of stopping criterion has proved effective in practice to prevent the overtraining of a network.

The ability of the network to generalize—that is, to classify correctly new, unknown pulp spectra—was tested on samples that had not been involved in the training (the test set). A network output greater than 0.5 was considered to indicate a pure raspberry pulp, while one below 0.5 was interpreted as non-raspberry. The trained network correctly classified 97 percent of the 280 samples in the test

117

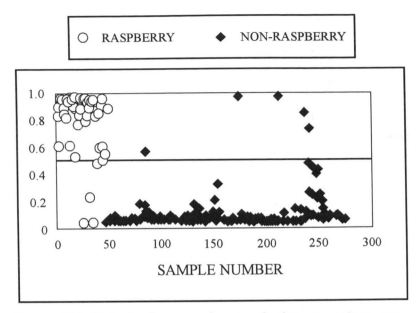

FIGURE III.6. Output of a neural network that recognizes pure raspberry pulp. A given sample is considered "pure raspberry" by the network if the output is greater than 0.5. Reprinted from *Food Testing and Analysis*, vol. 3, no. 3, June/July 1997, p. 24. Copyright © Target Group, Inc. Used with permission.

set. Figure III.6 shows the results of the classification. The output of the network is plotted against the sample code number (the symbols plotted represent the correct sample type).[17]

The power of the combination infrared spectroscopy/neural network lies in its expeditiousness: the mid-infrared spectrum of a fruit pulp sample can be collected in less than five minutes, and the network requires only a few seconds to deliver a prediction. A similar method had already been used to check the authenticity of coffee extracts.[18] (Rumors that the IFR team might have been approached by a drug cartel interested in their services are completely unfounded.)

Neural networks are not the only effective way to analyze spectra. Says Kate Kemsley, a member of the team that developed the new technique: "It was fun to try the neural approach, but I have to say, it wasn't essential in either case [raspberry or coffee] to use neural networks, as linear algebra methods worked just as well."

HAVE PROBLEM, WILL TRAVEL

The traveling salesman problem appeared in the United States during the 1930s, in connection with some practical questions coming from industry and management. In those post-depression years, the use of mathematical models to help make quantitative decisions was emerging as an independent branch of applied mathematics, later to be called operations research. Quite independently, the British developed their own operational research techniques during the Second World War, and applied them to the solution of a variety of problems concerning tactics, such as the efficient use of radar to track enemy aircraft.

Nobody seems to know precisely how the traveling salesman problem got its original name. Predictably, in the 1970s some attempted to rename it the traveling salesperson problem. But since the puzzle is now commonly referred to as the TSP, the sales rep's gender is conveniently no longer an issue.

What mathematicians currently call the TSP is a more general problem: given a set $\{1, 2, 3, \ldots, n\}$ of n "cities" and the "costs" $c(i, j)$ of traveling from city i to city j, find an ordering of the cities—that is, a tour—with minimum cost that visits each city exactly once (the cost of a tour is of course the sum of the costs of traveling from city to city in the given order). This relaxed version allows many variants. For example, intercity costs may not be the same in both directions; if they are, that is, if

$$c(i, j) = c(j, i),$$

we have a symmetric problem. Also, the so-called triangle inequality:

$$c(i, k) \leq c(i, j) + c(j, k),$$

which holds automatically when "costs" are real distances, may no longer be assumed. This means that the cost of going directly from city i to city k may exceed that of making a detour through city j. The distances between the vertices of any triangle satisfy the above inequality, hence its name. In what follows, we shall assume that the TSP refers to the original problem (a sales rep traveling from city to city), so the "costs" $c(i, j)$ are actual distances and the most economical tour is the shortest one.

In 1954, three mathematicians at RAND Corporation solved the first large-scale TSP borrowing methods from linear programming—a technique for solving certain optimization problems using a geometric approach. The problem was a "pure" TSP, for it involved real cities (Washington and 48 other large American cities). George Dantzig, Delbert Fulkerson, and Selmer Johnson represented each possible tour as a different vertex of a polyhedron in a "space" of more than 2,000 dimensions. With such a geometrical representation at hand, finding the shortest tour then becomes a standard linear programming problem.

The search for exact solutions of larger and larger TSPs soon developed into a kind of unofficial contest among researchers in the field. Needless to say, only nontrivial problems are accepted, typically those coming from printed circuit boards or other real-life applications. Over the years, the combined effect of improved algorithms and increased computing power resulted in one record after another being broken. The current world title has been claimed by a team of four American computer scientists[19] who in 1994 found the shortest tour of a 7,397-city problem.[20] Admittedly, their record-setting performance involved considerable computing resources: the algorithm needed an estimated three to four years of machine time on a network of computers to find the solution. But since the team ran their programs late at night, when the computers would have otherwise been idle, the actual cost was probably almost negligible. Whatever the case, in this particular contest speed or cost do not count as much as size—the number of cities involved. In real applications, however, computing time is a major factor, as is the requirement that the solution method should work for many instances of the problem and not just for one particular case.

THE NEURAL PATH TO OPTIMIZATION

How good are neural networks at solving optimization problems? As far as the indefatigable traveling rep is concerned, none of the existing neural solutions appears to be a match for more classical techniques. The famous traveling salesman puzzle is a natural choice

120

for testing an optimization method, but it is also a tricky one. Let us take a closer look.

The neural approach to the TSP was first proposed by Hopfield and D. W. Tank in 1985.[21] To solve an n-city problem, their method requires n^2 continuous neurons, each connected to all the others. We imagine the neurons disposed as an n-by-n square grid or matrix. Each neuron has a two-number label (i, j) indicating its position on the matrix: i-th row and j-th column. The state of neuron (i, j) is a variable x_{ij} that can take any value between 0 (nonfiring) and 1 (firing at maximum rate).

The state of the network at a given time t is completely described by the n^2 numbers x_{ij}. A value for x_{ij} between 0 and 1 represents the strength in the belief that city i is in position j of the tour. Possible solutions of the problem—that is, tours visiting each city once—are represented by certain binary matrices: a 1 in row i, column j, and 0s in the other positions of the row signify that city i is the j-th city to be visited. For example, a row 5 looking like this

$$0 \quad 0 \quad 1 \quad 0 \quad \cdots \quad 0 \quad 0$$

indicates that city 5 is the third in the tour. The matrix below encodes a tour that visits five cities in the order $2, 1, 5, 3, 4$

$$
\begin{array}{ccccc}
0 & 1 & 0 & 0 & 0 \\
1 & 0 & 0 & 0 & 0 \\
0 & 0 & 0 & 1 & 0 \\
0 & 0 & 0 & 0 & 1 \\
0 & 0 & 1 & 0 & 0.
\end{array}
$$

The length of a tour can be expressed as a function L (actually, a polynomial) of the n^2 variables x_{ij}. To guarantee that each city occurs only once in the tour, there should be exactly one firing neuron per row. This condition can be neatly written as the equation, or constraint:

$$\sum_{j=1}^{n} x_{ij} = 1, \text{ for each } i = 1, 2, \ldots, n.$$

121

The additional condition that each position j in the tour must be occupied by a single city leads to the second constraint

$$\sum_{i=1}^{n} x_{ij} = 1, \text{ for each } j = 1, 2, \ldots, n.$$

The traveling salesman problem can now be formulated as a so-called integer programming problem: Find integers x_{ij} satisfying the above constraints for which the value of the function L is a minimum. Hopfield and Tank's feedback network of continuous neurons—implemented as an analog circuit or simulated on a digital computer—attempts to solve precisely this problem. Its final (stable) state is the network's response which, once decoded into a tour, corresponds (hopefully) to the solution. Figure III.7 illustrates this neural solution for a 10-city problem.

To justify their use of continuous neurons, Hopfield and Tank invoke a need for flexible or "fuzzy" logical operations. "During an analog convergence," they write,[22] "several conflicting solutions or propositions can be simultaneously considered through the continuous variables. It is as though the logical operations of a calculation could be given continuous values between 'true' and 'false' and evolve toward certainty only near the end of the calculation. This is evident during the TSP convergence process (fig. III.7). [. . .] This use of a continuous variable between true and false is similar to the theory of fuzzy sets. Two-state neurons do not capture this computational feature."

An obvious drawback of the above approach is the magnitude of the computational demands: solving a 1,000-city problem requires one million neurons, each connected to all the others—one trillion connection weights! In a recent book,[23] David Johnson, of AT & T Labs and Lyle McGeoch, of Amherst College, evaluate and compare the various techniques for solving the TSP, including genetic algorithms and neural networks. They observe that although Hopfield and Tank regularly found optimal tours for 10-city instances, their networks "often failed to converge to feasible solutions [i.e., to a tour] when $n = 30$, and the best solutions they ever found on such an instance was still more than 17 percent above optimal."

A different approach, where neurons are viewed as points in the plane, can handle significantly larger instances. During the computation, the neurons (nicknamed "ants") gradually move toward the

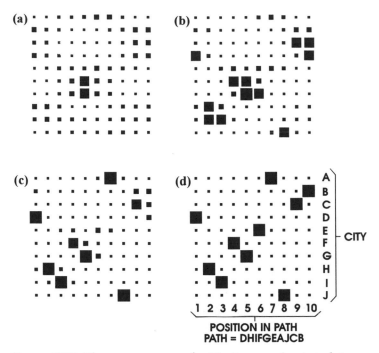

FIGURE III.7. The convergence of a 10-city neural network to a tour. The linear dimension of each square is proportional to the value of x_{ij}. (*a* to *c*) Intermediate times. (*d*) The final state. Indices illustrate how the final state is decoded into a tour (solution of the TSP). Reprinted with permission from "Computing with Neural Circuits: A Model," by John J. Hopfield and David W. Tank, *Science*, vol. 223, no. 4764, 8 August 1986, pp. 625–33. Copyright 1986 American Association for the Advancement of Science.

cities as if connected by a long loop of string. They eventually form a polygon that looks like a physical tour, each city being "occupied" by one neuron. Using such a "geometric" network, Shara Amin and José Luis Fernandez, of British Telecom, solved (with 4 percent accuracy) a randomly generated 30,000-city instance[24]—the largest solution ever found with this method at the time (1994).

The mathematics behind these geometric networks derives from ideas of Teuvo Kohonen, of the Helsinki University of Technology. In particular, his self-organizing maps[25] and the learning algorithm that goes with them, known as winner-take-all.[26] Kohonen's most original contributions to neural computing found successful applications in many fields, from speech recognition to robot control.

Johnson and McGeoch conclude their analysis of neural solutions for the TSP by questioning their practical value. But they do not pronounce themselves on the potential of neural optimization at large: "If the large body of research into refining these [neural] algorithms is to have any practical consequences, it will most likely have to be in other domains, where the lessons learned in the TSP domain might bear more useful fruit."[27]

NOTES

1. T. Kohonen, *Proceedings of the 3rd International Conference on Fuzzy Logic, Neural Nets and Soft Computing*, Iizuka, Japan, 1994, p. xiii.

2. W. S. McCulloch and W. Pitts, "A Logical Calculus of the Ideas Immanent in Nervous Activity," *Bull. Math. Biophys.* 5, 115–33 (1943).

3. F. Rosenblatt, "The Perceptron: A Probabilistic Model for Information Storage and Organisation in the Brain," *Psych. Rev.* 65, 386–408 (1958).

4. J. J. Hopfield, "Neural Networks and Physical Systems with Emergent Collective Computational Abilities," *Proc. Nat. Academy of Sci.* 79: 2554–58, 1982.

5. J. Zurada, D. M. Zigoris, P. B. Aronhime, and M. Desai, "Multi-Layer Feedforward Networks for Printed Character Classification," *Proc. 34th Midwest Symp. on Circuits and Systems*, Monterey, CA, May 14–16, 1991.

6. Fred Cohen, "Computer Viruses, Theory and Experiments." *Computers and Security*, vol. 6, pp. 22–35, 1987.

7. W. H. Murray, "The Application of Epidemiology to Computer Viruses." *Computers and Security*, vol. 7, pp. 130–50, 1988.

8. J. O. Kephart et al., "Biologically Inspired Defenses Against Computer Viruses." *International Conference on Artificial Intelligence*, 1995, pp. 985–96.

9. Fred Cohen, "Computer Viruses, Theory and Experiments." *Computers and Security*, vol. 6, pp. 22–35, 1987.

10. P. J. Werbos, "Beyond Regression: New Tools for Prediction and Analysis in the Behavioral Sciences," Doctoral Dissertation, Appl. Math., Harvard University, Mass., 1974.

11. J. J. Hopfield, "Neural Networks and Physical Systems with Emergent Collective Computational Abilities," *Proc. Natl. Acad. Sci. USA*, vol. 79, pp. 2554–58, April 1982, Biophysics.

12. Ibid.

13. Ibid.

14. R. E. Howard, L. D. Jackel, and H. P. Graf, 1988, "Electronic Neural Networks," *AT & T Tech. J.* (May): 58–64.

15. Jacek M. Zurada, *Introduction to Artificial Neural Systems*, West Publishing Co., 1992, p. 254.

16. M. Defernez, E. K. Kemsley, and R. H. Wilson, "Use of Infrared Spectroscopy and Chemometrics for the Authentification of Fruit Purees." *J. Agric. Food Chem.* 43, 109–13, 1995.

17. J. K. Holland, R. H. Wilson, and E. K. Kemsley, "Detecting Adulteration of Raspberry Pulps," *Food Testing and Analysis*, vol. 3, no. 3, 1997, pp. 20–22, 44.

18. R. Briandet, E. K. Kemsley, and R. H. Wilson, "Approaches to Adulteration Detection in Instant Coffees Using Infrared Spectroscopy and Chemometrics," *J. of the Science of Food & Agriculture* 71 (1996), 359–66.

19. David Applegate of AT & T Bell Labs, Robert Bixby of Rice University, Vasek Chvátal of Rutgers University, and William Cook of Bellcore.

20. David S. Johnson and Lyle A. McGeoch, "The Traveling Salesman Problem: A Case Study in Local Optimization," in *Local Search in Combinatorial Optimisation*, E.H.L. Aarts and J. K. Lenstra, eds., John Wiley & Sons, New York, 1997.

21. J. J. Hopfield and D. W. Tank, " 'Neural' Computation of Decisions in Optimization Problems," *Biol. Cybern.* 52 (1985), 141–52.

22. John J. Hopfield and David W. Tank, "Computing with Neural Circuits: A Model," *Science*, vol. 233, 8 Aug. 1986, pp. 625–33.

23. David S. Johnson and Lyle A. McGeoch, "The Traveling Salesman Problem: A Case Study in Local Optimization," in *Local Search in Combinatorial Optimisation*, E.H.L. Aarts and J. K. Lenstra, eds., John Wiley & Sons, New York, 1997, pp. 215–310.

24. S. Amin, "A Self-Organized Travelling Salesman," *Neural Computing and Applications* 2 (1994), 129–33.

25. T. Kohonen, "Self-Organization and Associative Memory." Berlin: Springer-Verlag, 1984.

26. T. Kohonen, "The 'Neural' Phonetic Typewriter," *IEEE Computer* 27(3): 11–22 (1988).

27. Johnson and McGeoch, "The TSP: A Case Study," note 20.

CHAPTER SIX

Solutions via Evolution

GENETICS

WHEN living organisms reproduce, offspring inherit their parents' characteristic features. Humans have babies, flies lay eggs which mature to become other flies, and apple seeds grow into apple trees. The specific traits that groups of organisms have in common determine a species. The term has a precise meaning for biologists, who have named and described over three million of them. But informally, a species is a group of individuals (plants, animals, insects, etc.) with very similar structure and behavior and able to breed with each other.

Species were once thought to be immutable, that is, each species of animal or plant could be seen in the present exactly as it had always been in the past. But some 150 years ago, in *On the Origin of Species by Means of Natural Selection*, the English naturalist Charles Darwin argued that all living organisms are the descendants of a few forms of life that appeared on Earth in the very distant past. (Darwin's theory, published in 1859, carried a subtitle more suggestive of a socially incorrect essay than a piece on natural science: "The Preservation of Favoured Races in the Struggle for Life.") Following Darwin's revolutionary theory, a species is now considered as a dynamically changing population of varying individuals, some of which may eventually evolve into a new species. The major mechanisms by which this evolution takes place are natural selection and mutation, both intimately connected with the process that enables the parents' characteristics to be passed on to their descendants.

The scientific study of how hereditary traits are transmitted from parents to offspring is known as genetics. The indisputable father of this branch of biology is the Austrian monk Gregor Mendel, who discovered its basic laws after observing garden pea plants reproduce. In the purest scientific spirit, he set up a series of clever experiments to test his hypotheses, and he was also one of the first to use mathematical concepts in biological inquiries. Mendel's ideas were definitely ahead of his time. His fundamental contribution was not recognized until 1900, sixteen years after his death and more than thirty years after the publication of his findings in a scientific journal. But if Mendel failed to convince his contemporaries, he remained persuaded that his conjectures were correct. "My time will come," he reportedly said shortly before his death.

And come it did. We know today that hereditary traits such as eye color in animals or the shape of a plant's leaves, are passed on to the next generation as discrete "units" or genes—Mendel's original idea. Genes are arranged in a precise order on certain parts of the nucleus of a cell called chromosomes, the physical carriers of hereditary information. The total number of genes in the cell varies from 5 or 10 (virus) to 100,000 (human cell). Each of these hereditary units contains biological information coded upon it—how to produce a specific protein, for example. The position of a gene in the chromosome is generally related to a particular function or feature of the organism, such as eye color. Uncommonly high blood pressure in some people has recently been linked to certain genes that researchers are trying to isolate.

The alternative forms of a same gene are its alleles. For instance, red and white are names for two alleles of the gene determining the eye color of fruit flies. Complex plant and animal life rely on a diploid or double-stranded genetic structure in which chromosomes occur in pairs. Each of the two homologous chromosomes in the pair contains information for the same functions. In a human cell there are 23 such pairs.

Anticipating the application of genetic ideas to computation, it is convenient to imagine an abstract "chromosome" as a finite string of n symbols representing the "genes." Each gene may appear in several forms—its alleles. For example, if the alleles are bits (0 or 1) then a chromosome is a binary word such as

$$1101100010110100.$$

Here $n = 16$; the first gene is 1 and the 15th gene is 0.

POPULATIONS AND NATURAL SELECTION

A population is a group of individuals of the same species, living and interbreeding in relative isolation from other groups—a colony of wild rabbits on a certain island, say. Because of reproduction and death, the composition of the group is constantly changing. Each member of the population possesses both a genotype and a phenotype. The former is the particular set of genes that the individual carries; the latter designates its actual physical appearance or visible characteristics. The relation between the two is a complex one, an individual's phenotype being determined by its inheritance (genotype) but also partly by its environment. It may seem obvious that genes exist for the sole purpose of making possible the reproduction of phenotypes. But some biologists have argued that nature's design is the other way around: birds, cows, and humans are the mechanisms their genes have devised to perpetuate themselves, that is, we exist for our genes, and not the opposite.

The population interacts with and is affected by its surroundings —climatic conditions, food supply, predators, other populations, and so forth. Since organisms vary in their physical characteristics (phenotype), some individuals (and their genes) are more likely to survive than others in a given environment. Thus, the environment implicitly selects who lives and who dies. To increase its chances of survival, the population has its own plan: adaptation. The price to pay for the failure to adapt is extinction.

Adaptation does not proceed in an arbitrary manner, by trying out phenotypes at random until hitting by chance on the best one. It is rather a gradual process, whereby good individuals are progressively modified to produce better individuals. Darwin defined natural selection as the preservation of favorable variations and the rejection of injurious ones. Thus, well-adapted organisms survive and reproduce, passing on valuable genetic information to their descendants, while poor performers are weeded out. Hence, the survival of the fittest, a key idea in Darwin's evolutionary arguments. (Since the "fitness" of an individual is measured by its skill to play the survival game, there is a tautology lurking here: Who survives? Those who are most fit to...survive.) Over many generations, the relative proportions of different phenotypes in the population will change in favor of the best adapted ones.

Since the physical carriers of heredity are the chromosomes, it is at that level that evolution works in order to modify the characteristics of individuals. Certain combinations of alleles for different genes can significantly augment the performance of the phenotype. Adaptation may thus be seen as a search for "good" allele associations through changes in the genetic makeup. Such genetic changes come about by way of processes in which chance plays a fundamental role. This fact is the guiding principle for the application of evolutionary ideas to computing.

The totality of chromosomes carried by the members of the population constitutes the chromosome (or gene) pool. This is usually an infinitesimally small fraction of all conceivable chromosomes. In the case of human chromosomes, to write down the number of possible varieties in decimal notation would require over two billion figures. It is convenient to imagine adaptation taking place in discrete time-steps or "generations." Thus, if $C(t)$ is the chromosome pool at a given time t, then $C(t + 1)$ is the totality of chromosomes in the population one generation later. In general, $C(t + 1)$ will contain new chromosomes as well as others already in $C(t)$, while some of the $C(t)$ chromosomes may get lost. New chromosomes may be created out of old ones in various ways: genetic elements may be lost, rearranged, exchanged, or added.

For the purpose of modeling evolution, the two most relevant processes of chromosomal variation are crossover and mutation. During crossover, segments of two different chromosomes switch places with one another, separating some traits and joining others into new—and possibly beneficial—associations (see fig. III.8). Such a swapping of genetic material happens when sperm and ova fuse. Mutations are changes in the genetic makeup of a chromosome that occur spontaneously during the reproduction of cells or are caused by radiation, chemicals, or other outside agents. Mutations add a touch of randomness to the variations in the gene pool, and without them evolution might be limited. The abstract counterparts of crossover and mutation play a fundamental role in the efficiency of the "genetic" algorithms about to be introduced.

MODELING EVOLUTION

Adaptation in natural populations aims at improving the fitness, and therefore the chances for survival, of the group as a whole. Computer models of evolution, on the other hand, are mostly concerned with "breeding" one exceptional individual, whose "genetic code" would represent the optimal or a near-optimal solution to a problem. But in order to increase the likelihood of such a desirable event, the model

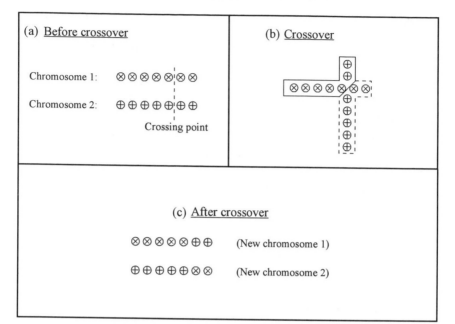

FIGURE III.8. Crossover. Segments of two different chromosomes switch places with one another.

must gradually improve the average quality of entire "generations" of potential solutions, just as in the biological case. We give below a very simple example of this process, leaving a detailed analysis of the model for later sections.

A problem consists in finding the integer x between 0 and 127 for which a mysterious function $f(x)$—to be revealed later—takes on its maximum value. Each of the numbers $0, 1, 2, \ldots, 126, 127$ is here a potential solution. In biological language, they are the possible phenotypes of the species. (To keep the example simple, we have restricted the number of solution candidates to just a few dozen. In any realistic application, their number would be astronomical. Then, trying to discover the maximum by the systematic calculation of all function values $f(x)$ would be out of the question.) The function f may be viewed as measuring the "fitness" of a potential solution x, that is, how well x fared in the "environment." The higher the score $f(x)$, the better the quality of a phenotype x. Our goal is then to find an x whose fitness is as high as possible.

The graph of f appears in figure III.9. As with any typical fitness function, it possesses several peaks and valleys. The highest peaks correspond to the best individuals—the optimal solutions. The other peaks are local maxima, or best solutions for values of x restricted to a certain neighborhood. We can see that there are two optimal solutions, $x = 42$ and $x = 85$. Of course, in any nontrivial problem the graph of the fitness function would be impossible to draw, let alone inspect, so we would have no clues regarding the identity of the fittest, or where to look for them. All we would be allowed to do is to test individual solutions for fitness and use this information as best we can to "breed" better solutions. In what follows, we illustrate a solution method assuming no knowledge of f other than the possibility of computing the values $f(x)$ one at a time, whenever we need them.

The strategy of a genetic algorithm is based on the mechanisms of natural selection and evolution. Its implementation normally requires considerable computing resources to store the data, automate the operations, and speed up the evolutionary clock. After some preliminary steps (coding, selecting the initial solution pool, etc.), the evolutionary plan proceeds in a cyclic fashion, producing a new "generation" of potential solutions after each cycle. A combination of chance and controlled "reproduction" will favor the development of first-rate solutions in the long run, perhaps after thousands of generations. But there is no guarantee that the model will actually deliver an optimal or near-optimal solution. The case for the plan's eventual success rests on statistical arguments rather than on exact mathematical proof. Nonetheless, there is ample experimental evidence that, given the right conditions, the model does work for certain types of problems. Here are the principal phases of the algorithm.

1. *Coding.* We first specify a "genetic code" for each potential solution x. This may be done by writing the number x in base 2. For example, if $x = 13$, then its code is the binary string 1101; if $x = 65$, its code is 1000001. (Binary coding is based on the powers of 2. Thus, 13 is represented by the binary string 1101 because $1 \times 2^3 + 1 \times 2^2 + 0 \times 2^1 + 1 \times 2^0 = 8 + 4 + 0 + 1 = 13$.)

2. *Initial Population.* A small set of strings is chosen at random from the solution pool to form the initial population, or generation 0, and each x on this set has its fitness $f(x)$ evaluated. The composition of an initial population of six strings is given below.

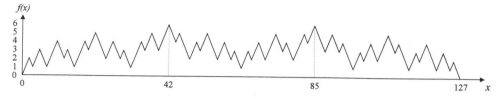

FIGURE III.9. The graph of a mysterious function.

Generation 0 (initial population)

Phenotype	Code (*genotype*)	Fitness ($= f(x_i)$)
$x_1 = 5$	$s_1 = 0000101$	3
$x_2 = 38$	$s_2 = 0100110$	4
$x_3 = 11$	$s_3 = 0001011$	3
$x_4 = 24$	$s_4 = 0011000$	2
$x_5 = 112$	$s_5 = 1110000$	1
$x_6 = 79$	$s_6 = 1001111$	2
	Total fitness	15

3. *Cloning.* Two or more strings from the current population are chosen at random to "mate." To favor the reproduction of the best performing individuals, the probability that a string be chosen is proportional to its fitness. In the above example, the fitness of string s_2 is twice that of string s_6. Therefore, s_2 has twice as many chances as s_6 of being selected. Copies, or clones, of the selected strings are made and all these constitute the reproduction pool.

4. *Reproduction.* The mating strings (s_1 and s_2, say) exchange segments of consecutive genes by crossover to create two children; e.g., they may swap their last three genes:

Parents	Children
0000101	0000110
0100110	0100101

The length and position of the segments to be exchanged is determined by chance every time a coupling takes place. In the above example, the strings swapped genes no. 5 to no. 7.

132

5. *Population Updating.* The offspring resulting from the mating replace either low-fitness strings or members of the population chosen at random, depending on the particular updating schema chosen. If we suppose that the strings to be replaced are s_1 and s_6, then the composition of the next generation is shown below (a decoding procedure is applied to each string prior to the calculation of its fitness).

Generation 1

Code (Genotype)	Decoded String (x)	Fitness (= f(x))
0000110	6	2
0100110	38	4
0001011	11	3
0011000	24	2
1110000	112	1
0100101	37	5
Total fitness		17

Observe that in this new generation a solution of fitness 5 has appeared ($x = 37$), the best solution to date. Also, the average fitness of the population is now 2.83 ($= 17/6$), better than the 2.50 average of the previous generation. However, these local improvements after just one generation are not significant, nor are they any indication that the model works as intended. It is only after many repetitions of steps 3 to 5 that the procedure is likely to generate a highly fit string. We shall analyze later the underlying assumptions and possible explanations for the expected success of the model.

LESSONS AND QUESTIONS

We now disclose the true nature of the fitness function whose graph is displayed in figure III.9. What appears to be an arbitrary function actually counts the number of times 0s and 1s alternate in the genetic code of x. More precisely, the fitness of x is the number of occurrences of the substrings "01" or "10" in the string representing x. For instance, $f(34) = 4$ because in the encoding of 34, namely, 0100100,

"01" and "10" occur twice each. Therefore, the quality (fitness) of a phenotype x is conveniently reflected in its genetic code.

Now, this is a rather exceptional situation, due to the artificial nature of our problem. In a real application—when the strings encode computer programs, for instance—there would be no simple way to determine which combinations of alleles correspond to high-quality solutions. Only time and the environment would tell. If we knew it from the outset, we could then build the optimal strings right away and there would be no need to simulate evolution. In other words, natural selection could be replaced by genetic engineering. In the above example, had we known that the more 0s and 1s intertwine the better the string, we would have come up right away with the fittest strings by alternating at every position: 1010101 (which corresponds to the phenotype $x = 85$) and 0101010 ($x = 42$).

Even in the presence of a favorable coding scheme, there is one element that may prevent the plan from breeding an optimal solution: the lack of enough genetic diversity. The above model creates new genetic combinations by crossover, but if all the strings in the initial population happen to have the same allele in a certain position, this genetic trait will persist through all future generations. For example, if all strings in the initial pool end with 0, then no amount of crossing-over will ever produce a string ending with 1. In particular, the optimal solution 1010101 could not be generated. In case the last two positions of every initial string are 0s, both optimal solutions would be beyond the evolutionary range. Inspired by nature, evolutionary algorithms generally incorporate a mutation operator as an insurance against genetic stagnation.

Our simple example has illustrated the highlights of genetic algorithms:

Coding. Potential solutions are represented by their "genetic code," e.g., as binary strings.

Solution pool. A small number of strings form a "population" of potential solutions which the algorithm uses to search for better solutions.

Performance testing. The quality of a solution is evaluated by a "fitness" number.

Variation. New genetic combinations are created, e.g., by crossover ("sexual reproduction").

Selection. Good performers are more likely to reproduce than poor ones.

Evolution. The newly created individuals replace some (or all) existing strings to form the next generation.

Non-Determinism. Certain operations involve random choices or rules based on probability.

Mutation. Random (but infrequent) local changes may occur in the genetic code to increase diversity.

Variation, selection, evolution. An alluring strategy, especially when we are facing a problem for which no efficient solution method is known. But many questions linger: What is a suitable coding of solutions? How can we measure fitness? How long will it take for an optimal or near-optimal solution to appear and how do we recognize it? And, particularly, will the scheme work at all? These are very good questions indeed, so good that the only honest answer we have for all of them is: in general, we don't know. This does not mean that there are no partial answers, or even complete and very satisfactory answers in some cases, as we shall demonstrate in the coming sections.

THE MATHEMATICAL FRAMEWORK

Theory should provide us with means of prediction and
control not directly suggested by compilations of data
or simple tinkering.
(John H. Holland)[1]

Cross-breeding and natural selection occur spontaneously throughout the living world. Having understood their function, humans have long artificially replicated these processes to create better crops and exotic flowers. The mechanism of biological evolution also inspired an American mathematician, but for a different purpose than to develop superior organisms. His aim in emulating nature's plan was to "breed" efficient solutions to problems, especially some complex problems that do not generally yield to traditional solution methods.

John Holland may be better described as a polymath, or multidisciplinary scientist. He holds degrees in physics, mathematics, and communication sciences, and is a professor of psychology and of electrical engineering and computer science at the University of Michigan. The publication in 1975 of his book *Adaptation in Natural and Artificial Systems*[2] marked the official launching of the genetic

135

algorithm, a technique to simulate evolution on a computer he had begun developing in the 1960s. Holland's book set up a mathematical framework for the theoretical study and practical implementation of adaptive strategies. These processes play a critical role not only in biology, but also in domains as diverse as psychology, economics, computational mathematics, and artificial intelligence.

As it had been the case with the notion of a fuzzy set, it took some time before the new idea's potential was fully appreciated. For several years, research in adaptive systems remained mostly confined to Holland and his students, until interest in his techniques began to spread around the mid-1980s. The number of researchers presently studying genetic algorithms is estimated at several hundred, and an interdisciplinary consortium, the Santa Fe Institute, is dedicated to the study of complex adaptive systems ranging from economies to ecologies. To give the reader some feeling for how genetic algorithms work we shall resort to some geometric metaphors.

Space Search

The use of a genetic algorithm to solve a given problem requires some preliminary operations, beginning with the encoding of the potential solutions in a format that resembles the way information is packed in a chromosome—a popular choice is to represent each solution candidate as a binary string. It is also necessary to evaluate in some reasonable sense the "quality" of solutions. This is usually done by assigning to each possible solution a single number, its fitness or payoff value, in effect ranking the solutions on a linear scale. Choosing a suitable coding scheme and fitness function is not as easy as it may sound, and they are perhaps the most crucial and most difficult parts of the process.

Let us imagine the collection of all solutions forming a plane surface, each solution (encoded as a binary string) becoming a point in this plane. (Although a convenient image, such a representation presupposes that the set of potential solutions has a rather simple structure.) This plane surface is called the search space. By searching through its points we expect to locate the strings with high fitness that encode the best solutions to our problem (we shall speak of "points" or "strings" indifferently). It is worth recalling that the number of possible solutions is normally so large that a systematic, string-by-string search is out of the question.

Imagine now a second, irregular surface, resembling a landscape of peaks and valleys and floating over the search space. Sitting directly above each string s there is a point on this landscape. The distance separating the two is proportional to the fitness of s; the higher the point, the better the quality of the solution encoded by s. Our goal is to locate the strings above which the fitness surface is as high as possible. This would be easy if we could actually "see" the landscape's summits. But naturally we can't, so the search must be conducted entirely at ground level, that is, through properties of the strings themselves.

Since the initial "population" of strings is chosen at random, these strings will be haphazardly distributed throughout the search space. The genetic algorithm's design is to force future "generations" to be mostly composed of strings in the high-fitness regions of the space. The key to the algorithm's efficiency is its implicit parallelism, a property which allows it to explore vast regions of the search space while manipulating relatively few strings.

Schemata

One of the fundamental assumptions supporting a genetic algorithm is that the secret of a string's success is hidden in its genetic code, although we may never know exactly where. By exploiting the structural similarities among strings with high fitness, the algorithm increases the chance for strings with even higher fitness to appear. And so, patterns of allele combinations, known as schemata (singular, "schema"), play a central role in the search strategy. The algorithm's long-term goal is to foster the proliferation of "good" schemata among the string population.

A schema is a particular configuration of alleles in certain positions of a string. For instance, the schema 0 0 $*$ $*$ 1 $*$ $*$ $*$ $*$ 1 stipulates that the string must begin with two 0s and have a 1 in the fifth and tenth positions; the asterisk ($*$) in the remaining places is meant as a "don't care" symbol, that is, either allele—0 or 1—may appear there. Every schema describes a certain region of the search plane, namely, the set of those strings which match the schema at the specified positions. The above schema has 6 "don't care" positions; therefore it describes a set of 64 ($= 2^6$) strings, which includes 000011111 and 0001110001 but not 010011111. (The number 64 was obtained by the application of a counting principle. Readers not familiar with these techniques are not missing anything significant here or elsewhere in the book—except perhaps the possibility of checking our calculations by themselves.)

Conversely, a given string of length k is an instance of 2^k different schemata. For example, 1001101000 is described by 2^{10} ($= 1,024$) schemata. These include $1 * * * * * * * * *$, $10 * * * * * * * 0$, $* 0 0 * 1 0 1 * * *$, and so forth. As Holland observed, in computing the fitness of a string we are also deriving information on the 2^k schemata that describe the string. In particular, a high-quality string provides information on the possible location of high-fitness regions of the search space. This feature of the algorithm—the testing of many schemata by testing a single string—amounts to having many computations taking place in parallel.

There is a notion of fitness associated with each schema, namely, the average fitness value of all strings in the population that match the schema. In selecting strings for mating with probability proportional to their fitness, the algorithm favors the reproduction of schemata with high fitness. Thus, behind the scenes of the changing string population, a concurrent search is taking place in pursuit of the best performing schemata. Using probabilistic arguments, Holland has estimated how the number of strings matching a given schema is expected to change from one generation to the next. In his schemata theorem, also called the Fundamental Theorem of Genetic Algorithms, he demonstrates that a schema will proliferate all the more rapidly if, apart from having high fitness, it contains a small number of specific alleles and these are very close together. For example, $* * 1 * 0 1 * * * *$ contains three specific alleles which spread over four positions. The small spread reduces the probability of the schema being disrupted during crossover.

Short sequences of genes with particular values are called building blocks. "Good" building blocks are those whose presence in a chromosome is a statistical telltale of the chromosome's high fitness. By favoring the recombination of the fittest strings, the algorithm increases the probability for good building blocks from different chromosomes to end up in the same one. Assuming that the association of good building blocks is a good thing, outstanding strings are then likely to appear given enough time. But since time means computer time and this commodity comes at a price, there is a practical limit to how long the algorithm may be allowed to run. If we are to appreciate the margin between theory and practice, it is perhaps time we meet a real application.

PRISONER'S DILEMMA

> Instead of asking a complicated question (as all
> psychologically important questions must be) and
> coming up with a very simple answer (often in the form
> of yes, no, or maybe), one might try asking a very
> simple question (such as, "given a choice between two
> alternatives what will a person do?") and derive a rich
> and complex avalanche of answers.
> *(Mathematician Anatol Rapoport, reflecting on the method of*
> *experimental psychology)*[3]

Prisoner's Dilemma is the nickname given to a simple two-person game that has no satisfactory solution, in the sense that the rational strategy leads to an outcome that is worse for both players than if they choose their options "irrationally." The name was inspired by the hypothetical plight of two suspects of a crime who are being held in separate cells. The police promises each of them immunity in exchange for testimony against the other. While it is in the individual interest of each prisoner to confess, regardless of what the other does, it is in their collective interest to keep mum.

The rules of the game are simple enough. Each player has two cards labeled *C* (for cooperation) and *D* (as in defection). A trial consists in both persons playing (simultaneously) one of their two cards. There is a payoff associated with each trial, which may be a reward or a penalty, depending on who played what. If both players play card *C*, they each receive 8 points; if, instead, they both play *D*, each loses 3 points. In case they happen to play different cards, the *D*-card player earns 10 points while the one who played *C* receives a 10-point penalty. Needless to say, the players are not allowed to communicate with each other in any way. An agreed number of trials played in succession (one hundred, say) constitutes a game.

The various payoffs may be interpreted in the light of the situation that inspired the game's name. If prisoner *A*, say, yields to temptation and cuts a deal while B refuses to confess, then temptation pays off and A is released ($T = +10$ points for A), while B—the "sucker" —gets a stiff sentence ($S = -10$ points for B). If both confess, they get away with a lighter punishment ($P = -3$ points each) for collaborating with the police. But if neither of the two caves in, the police does not have a case and must set both of them free. The suspects are then rewarded by cooperating with each other ($R = +8$ points each).

Knowledge of the payoff rules does not permit any of the two players to devise an a priori winning strategy. The consequence of one player's choice of card—whether it will result in a reward or a penalty—depends on the other's unpredictable move. Nevertheless —and this is an interesting aspect of the game—the history of past trials, known to both players, may be used to guide their future decisions. In the technical jargon of the theory of games, a zero-sum game is one in which a player may only benefit at the expense of the other; more precisely, one person's gain equals the other's loss, so the (algebraic) sum of the points allotted to both players on any given trial is always zero. Prisoner's Dilemma is therefore not a zero-sum game, since both players can earn (or lose) points on a given trial.

The number of temptation (T), sucker (S), punishment (P), and reward (R) points may be allocated in many different ways, and the playing strategies will vary accordingly. This was confirmed by a series of experiments conducted at the University of Michigan in the 1960s, with students hired as players. One of the experiments, for example, showed that when the reward for cooperation was increased from $R = 1$ to $R = 9$ while the other payoffs were kept constant, the average frequency of playing card C (i.e., cooperating) increased from 46 to 73 percent of the time.

PLAYING THE GAME

Prisoner's Dilemma has been used by psychologists to study human behavior in situations involving cooperation-defection alternatives, and by political scientists interested in the dynamics of international conflict. Computer tournaments have pitted different playing strategies against one another. The game plan "tit for tat" is one of the most effective known strategies, despite its disarming simplicity: it begins by cooperating on the opening move and thereafter plays whatever the opponent did on the previous trial, that is, it rewards cooperation by cooperating and it punishes defection by defecting. Tit for tat was the overall winner in a computer contest organized in 1979 by Robert Axelrod, a political scientist and conflict resolution expert at the University of Michigan. The 62 contending strategies, some of which were quite intricate, were submitted by game theory experts, computer buffs, and professors in various scientific disciplines. For good measure, the leave-it-to-chance strategy—play C or D at random with equal probability—was also included. They were all beaten by the unsophisticated tit for tat, proposed by mathematician Anatol Rapoport.

The success of such a simple playing scheme intrigued Axelrod, who wondered whether other equally powerful strategies could be discovered with the help of a genetic algorithm. He began by formulating the possible strategies in the form of decision rules. Each of these rules stipulates the player's move based on the outcomes of the three previous trials. The strategies were then encoded as binary strings (chromosomes) as is explained below.

Any given trial has four possible outcomes: CC, CD, DC, and DD, since each person may play either C or D. If we represent these outcomes by R, S, T, and P, respectively, then a sequence of three trials becomes a string of three letters. For instance, DC, DC, CC becomes TTR. Each of these 64 ($= 4^3$) strings may be interpreted as a number from 0 to 63 written in base 4 arithmetic, with the following correspondence between letters and numerals: $R = 0$, $S = 1$, $T = 2$, and $P = 3$. In this way, each 3-trial sequence is assigned a rank between 0 and 63. For example, the sequence of trials DC, DC, CC is first written as the string TTR and then becomes 220 (in base 4), which in turn decodes (in base 10) as $2 \times 4^2 + 2 \times 4^1 + 0 \times 1 = 32 + 8 + 0 = 40$ ($=$ the sequence's rank).

For each 3-trial sequence there is a rule dictating the player's next move. For instance, $TTR \rightarrow D$ means: if the sequence TTR has been played, then play D. A particular strategy is then a set of 64 rules (the genes) which is coded as a binary word (a chromosome). Each bit encodes the player's response, 0 ($= C$) or 1 ($= D$), and its position within the word corresponds to the rank of the 3-trial sequence previously played. An example will illustrate the coding principle:

Rank:	0	1	2	...	40	...	62	63
Bit:	1	0	0	...	1	...	0	1.

The above binary word decodes as the following set of rules (strategy):

Rank	Last 3 Plays		Move
0	RRR	→	D
1	RRS	→	C
2	RRT	→	C
...	...		...
...	...		...
40	TTR	→	D
...	...		...
62	PPT	→	C
63	PPP	→	D.

Actually, each binary word also contains six other bits to represent the assumed behavior of the players at the game's opening (i.e., during the first three trials). Thus, 0 1 1 0 0 0 would indicate that the presumed outcomes of the first three trials were CD, DC, and CC in that order. Each chromosome is therefore a 70-bit word, whose first six genes (bits) represent opening game moves and the rest encode a particular strategy. A quick calculation shows that the total number of chromosomes (i.e., the size of the search space) exceeds 10^{21}, which is about ten thousand times the estimated age of the universe in seconds.

Notice that in the present situation chromosomes do not represent solutions to a problem but encode rules of behavior. In a sense, we *are* trying to solve a problem: that of getting a machine to learn how to play the game (and win). But unlike a typical optimization problem, machine learning does not have a well-defined optimal solution. The situation resembles the adaptation of real organisms to a hostile environment. While some individuals adapt better than others (they may, for example, run faster), there is no absolute measure of fitness or a notion of "best" phenotype. Similarly, the fitness of Axelrod's chromosomes cannot be evaluated by a precise mathematical formula. The quality of a particular strategy for playing the game can only be tested by ... playing the game.

The Evolution of Strategies

Axelrod set up an "environment" to put strategies, or rather the strings encoding them, to the test. Eight opponents were chosen from the computer tournament entries as typical representatives of the 62 contenders. Each of these 8 strategies played a 151-trial game against the string S to be evaluated. The fitness of S was then calculated as the weighted average of the points scored by S in each of the 8 games (the weights were chosen to reflect the opponents' relative force, as measured by their ranking in the tournament).

Working with a population of only 20 strings—remember that there are quintillions of them—and after only 50 generations, the genetic algorithm was able to learn sets of rules whose average performance was as successful as tit for tat, the previous title-holder. And in 11 of the 40 runs (50 generations constitute a run) some strategies even beat tit for tat. Axelrod himself marveled at the result: "In these eleven runs, the population evolved strategies that manage to exploit one of the eight representatives [opponents] at the cost of achieving somewhat less cooperation with two others. But the net effect is a gain in effectiveness." And he goes on: "This is a remarkable achievement because to be able to get this added effectiveness, a rule [i.e., a strategy] must be able to do three things. First, it must be able to discriminate between one representative and another based upon only the behavior the other player shows spontaneously or is provoked into showing. Second, it must be able to adjust its own behavior to exploit a representative that is identified as an exploitable player. Third, and perhaps most difficult, it must be able to achieve this discrimination and exploitation without getting into too much trouble with the other representatives. This is something that none of the rules originally submitted to the tournament were able to do."[4]

But Axelrod also warns that while the genetic algorithm did manage to find highly effective rules, these strategies had evolved in a particular environment (the one made up of the eight strategies selected from the computer tournament) and may not be as "robust" as tit for tat in other environments. "In sum," he concludes, "the genetic algorithm is very good at what actual evolution does so well: developing highly specialized adaptations to specific environmental settings."

TEACHING MACHINES TO LEARN

The success of a genetic algorithm in finding winning strategies for Prisoner's Dilemma should not be entirely surprising. They had already demonstrated their power in similar circumstances by helping to program some classifier systems. These are sets of rules, roughly comparable to the more familiar expert systems, for performing specific tasks such as recognizing patterns. The rules in a classifier system form a population that evolves on the basis of stimuli and reinforcement from its environment. The purpose of this evolution is to "learn" which responses are most appropriate to a given stimulus.

One of the primary reasons for developing the earlier genetic algorithms was precisely to design machines that could learn how to do such nonmechanical things as recognize objects, make decisions, and control processes. Since no one knew how to program a computer to perform any of these tasks, it was a natural step to try to equip the machine with the ability to learn by itself. This is the fundamental idea behind the neural networks that we have met in the previous chapter.

The design of learning systems was also behind the first practical application of fuzzy logic. In the early 1970s, at London's Queen Mary College, Abe Mamdani and his student Seto Assilian were trying to simulate a simple industrial machine (a steam engine) with a computer program, while another program would try to learn how to operate the engine by trial and error. The controlling program, so the theory went, would do better and better by learning from its mistakes. Unfortunately (or perhaps fortunately), the scheme did not work as expected, even after the researchers had replaced the simulation with the actual machine. And so they abandoned the idea of a learning system and decided to try another approach: they wrote up a few heuristic rules for controlling the system and then used Zadeh's notion of a fuzzy set to encode the rules into a computer program. The machine was thus directly provided with the rule-of-thumb, practical knowledge of a human operator. This technique turned out to be amazingly effective, paving the way for the numerous future applications of fuzzy control.

Genetic algorithms and neural networks differ in their approach to the design of machines that can learn to perform "intelligent" tasks. While the former favor the emergence of the best strategies through competition, selection, and evolution, neural networks learn from examples and experience, with or without human supervision. Fuzzy systems, on the other hand, generate strategies based not on experience but on their ability to comprehend instructions; their knowledge is therefore communicated rather than acquired.

IQ AND FITNESS

What is intelligence? There is no shortage of answers to this fascinating question, which only proves that philosophers, psychologists, and scientists in general are still looking for the right one. Geneticist Daniel Cohen estimates that the word intelligence describes the faculty of understanding our environment, and so it is a relative notion because it depends on our upbringing. For Alain Connes, French mathematician and 1982 Fields medallist (the mathematicians' Nobel prize), the concept of intelligence defies a general definition. As for IQ tests, he believes that they only evaluate the subject's ability to guess what the test's authors consider to be expressions of intelligence.

Whatever it is precisely, intelligence might have to do not just with the things brains (human or otherwise) can do but also with the way they do them. Some human calculators can perform complex arithmetic operations in an incredibly short time; they don't seem to follow any scheme, the result just pops up in their mind after a few seconds. Impressive as it might be, such a skill would not normally be considered as a proof of "intelligence." Deep Blue, IBM's chess-playing computer, managed to beat the best opposition humankind had to offer—Russian champion Garry Kasparov. But the manner in which the machine performed its feat was anything but intelligent. Before making a move, Deep Blue's program ponders millions of possible options, even if at any one game situation there are only a dozen or so moves really worth considering. Systematically going through several million maneuvers just to rule them out is not our idea of cleverness. Not to mention the fact that the computer has to be told that a queen is more valuable than a knight and other equally obvious things that it is not "intelligent" enough to discover by itself.

Although Deep Blue did beat Kasparov in the opening game of their 1996 match, the world champion remained undefeated for the rest of the match, winning three games and tying the other two. It is not surprising that Kasparov eventually got the upper hand. For all its portentous memory and speed, the machine was in the end outsmarted by the human player's accumulated knowledge of its mechanical—hence predictable—playing style. Deep Blue's program must nonetheless contain some built-in unpredictability. Otherwise, by repeating the moves which once led to victory, its opponent would win every future game.

In the 1997 rematch things turned out differently, with the machine (no doubt helped by a souped-up program) getting the best of Kasparov. This outcome was variously greeted as a sad day for humanity, the end of the game of chess, and similar apocalyptic interpretations. Many had perhaps failed to notice that the match was really a confrontation between human beings: Kasparov versus the IBM team, each side disposing of vastly different means (consistent with this point of view is the fact that a human—not the machine—made the actual moves on the chessboard).

Not knowing exactly what intelligence is did not deter some people from trying to measure it. In 1904, the British psychologist Charles Spearman used statistical techniques to identify a number that he called the general factor of intelligence. According to Spearman, this number, known as g, captures a real property in the head and can be reasonably measured by IQ tests designed for that purpose. Of course not all psychometricians, let alone social scientists and other thinkers, support this point of view. The skeptics reject g as a fiction, the product of a particular mathematical representation of experimental data.

In *The Mismeasure of Man*,[5] the famous biologist Stephen Jay Gould argues against the fallacy of regarding intelligence as an innate, single-scaled thing in the head. He closes the chapter on the unreality of g by quoting John Stuart Mill: "The tendency has always been strong to believe that whatever received a name must be an entity or being, having an independent existence of its own. And if no real entity answering to the name could be found, men did not for that reason suppose that none existed, but imagined that it was something particularly abstruse and mysterious."

The premise that a certain quality can be seized by a single number underpins the notion of fitness, a central idea of genetic algorithms. Even if one accepts the principle, precisely how this number may be calculated remains a major hurdle in many practical situations. Similar questions arise almost every time mathematical models are constructed. Ultimately, the issue of whether or not it makes sense to measure a complex attribute on a linear scale is decided less by philosophical considerations than by the performance of the model.

IF YOU CAN'T SOLVE THEM, APPROXIMATE THEM

Mathematicians will only consider the traveling salesman problem as solved the day someone finds an efficient algorithm that could calculate (at least in principle) the shortest tour for instances of arbitrary large size. But since the problem has been proved to be *NP*-complete (a notion explained in chapter 3), most experts are convinced that no such sweeping solution exists, so they have turned to constructing algorithms that compute good approximations in a reasonable time. One of the reasons the solution of the record-breaking 7,397-city problem required years of computing was that, since the algorithm had to calculate an optimal tour, most of the running time was devoted to checking optimality—yet another practical confirmation that precision is costly. Approximate methods, on the other hand, aim at calculating a tour that may be somewhat longer than the shortest one but which can be obtained in relatively little time, even for large numbers of cities. In most applications, such approximate solutions are virtually as good as the elusive optimal answer—and certainly much more cost-effective.

Strategies or sets of rules designed to find near-optimal tours rather than exact solutions are known as heuristics. A simple example is the nearest-neighbor heuristic, which is based on the commonsense rule of always traveling to the nearest city not already called upon: start at any city; choose as the second city the one closest to the first; choose as the third city the one closest to the second and not already visited; and so on. When you have finished visiting every city, complete the tour by returning to your starting point. The heuristic is usually accompanied by some sort of analysis that permits the user to estimate the quality of the approximation. For example, if there are 10^n cities, the nearest-neighbor heuristics constructs a tour that is guaranteed to be no more than $(n + 1)/2$ times the length of the optimal tour. For 100 cities, this means an approximate solution that is, at worst, 50 percent longer than the shortest tour (but in practice it is usually only around 25 percent off target). The best tour-construction heuristics, which gradually build a solution by some kind of growth process, can get within roughly 10 to 15 percent of the optimal tour in a relatively short time.

A still better performance is provided by the so-called local optimization techniques, which consist in repeatedly improving an approximate solution by making local changes. A classic in this category is an algorithm invented by Shen Lin and Brian Kernigham of Bell Labs in the early 1970s.[6] It—or some of its enhanced versions—can compute solutions for problems of up to one million cities that are typically only 1 to 2 percent off the optimal. Another famous, and more straightforward, example of local optimization is the 2-Opting heuristic. Starting with a given tour, it constructs a new one by an inversion or 2-Opt swap, which consists in reversing the order of two or more consecutive cities. For instance, if 4 5 6 1 2 8 7 3 represents the initial tour of eight cities, inverting the order of the last four cities results in the new tour 4 5 6 1 3 7 8 2. The only condition on the choice of the cities is that the inversion should produce a shorter tour. Geometrically, a 2-Opt swap first removes two edges from the graph representing the tour and then reconnects the two pieces in the other possible way (fig. III.10). The algorithm continues to perform 2-Opt swaps on the successively shorter tours until no further swaps can be made that would decrease the tour's length.

Local Traps

The quality of the final solution obtained by the application of the 2-Opt heuristic depends largely on the quality of the starting tour. This is a common drawback of many optimization techniques (on a wide range of problems, not just TSP) known as the local minimum trap. Figure III.11 schematically illustrates the situation. Imagine that you are exploring, blindfolded, an unknown landscape in search of the bottom of its lowest valley. A local search technique may be compared to testing only nearby points and moving in the direction of the steepest descent. If you happen to start the search at point A, you would then be lured into descending the slope leading to point B. Once you reach B, no further improvement is possible, for now you can only go up. The search would then stop, regardless of whether lower points, such as C, exist elsewhere. The point B is called a local minimum because it is the lowest point in a certain region. The true, or global, minimum is C—the lowest point in the

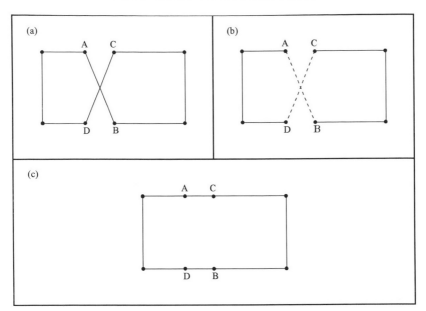

FIGURE III.10. A 2-Opt swap. (*a*) Original tour. (*b*) Edges *AB* and *CD* are removed, leaving two disjoint paths. (*c*) The two paths are reconnected in the other possible way, resulting in a shorter tour.

whole space. The global minimum is also a local minimum, but the converse is generally false. Complicated "landscapes," arising from practical problems, may have thousands of these deceptive local minima.

As a way of getting around local traps for the TSP, Shen Lin[7] suggested, back in 1965, the simple idea of repeating the local search many times, starting each time from a randomly chosen tour, until one was confident that all the locally optimal tours had been found. When Lin's idea of repeated local searches is combined with the genetic operators of selection, crossover, and mutation, one obtains a computation scheme that has produced some of the best-performing algorithms for the TSP.

GENETIC ALGORITHMS AND THE TSP

The first serious attempt to use genetic strategies for solving the traveling salesman problem dates from the mid-1980s, when R. M. Brady at Cavendish Laboratory in Cambridge, UK, applied what he

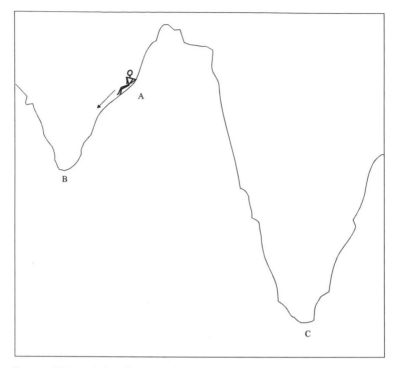

FIGURE III.11. A local trap. The descent from point *A* ends at the local minimum *B*. The global minimum (*C*) is elsewhere.

termed "optimization strategies gleaned from biological evolution" to a modest 64-city instance of the problem.[8] One of Brady's schemes consisted in repeatedly improving a starting tour by what amounts to attempted mutations: a section of the route is chosen at random and the order of visiting the cities is reversed, but only if this shortens the tour. Brady obtained a better performance by dividing the computation time between two independent trial solutions and selecting the best of the two at the end of the run. In order to evaluate the effect of competition, he later modified this scheme so that, at regular intervals, the better of the two solutions replaced the weaker one. "Surprisingly," he writes "this competitive strategy was far worse than the noncompetitive one. Our interpretation is that success at an early stage in the optimization was not closely correlated with success later on, because diversity was reduced." And he concluded by observing that "if a strategy is to favor the more successful solution it should be designed not to severely reduce diversity." The lesson to be learned here is that an evolutionary plan that helps weak individuals to survive may have a long-term advantage.

THE MATING GAME

If tours are coded in a straightforward way, that is, as lists of cities, an ordinary crossover will in general not produce a new—longer or shorter—tour but rather no tour at all. For example, exchanging the last two "genes" of 12348756 and 76813245, yields 12348745 and 76813256, respectively. In both of the new lists one city is missing and another one occurs twice, so that neither offspring represents a legal tour.

Many ways of avoiding the creation of illegal tours as a result of mating have been proposed. Brady's solution was first to search through both parent strings for substrings visiting the same cities in a different order and varying in length from 8 to 32 (if no such substrings were found, mating simply did not take place). For example, 123465789 and 925436871 both contain substrings involving cities 2, 3, 4, 5, and 6. Next, the lengths of the paths visiting these cities are calculated and the substring with the shorter one replaces the other. Referring to the above example, suppose that the distance 23 + 34 + 46 + 65 is found to be shorter than 25 + 54 + 43 + 36; then the two offsprings would be 123465789 (unchanged) and 923465871. Mating was attempted infrequently—once for every 2,000 random mutations —because of the considerable amount of computing time involved in searching for possible crossing-over points.

A more sophisticated mating strategy was devised by three computer scientists as part of what has been called "a major leap in genetic algorithm performance."[9] In 1988, H. Mühlenbein, M. Georges-Schleuter, and O. Krämer[10] introduced a new genetic algorithm for the TSP which they used to find an approximate solution of a 442-city problem—the best solution yet for that particular problem. Their algorithm was designed for implementation on a parallel computer, with each chromosome (i.e., each tour) in the population being assigned to a different processor.

AN IDEA WHOSE TIME HAS COME BACK

No idea is ever examined in all its ramifications and no
view is ever given all the chances it deserves.
(Philosopher of science Paul Feyerabend)[11]

Before describing Mühlenbein's scheme in more detail, let us go back to the biological ideas that inspired the original genetic algorithms. One of the basic principles was that only the information contained in the parent's genes can be passed on to their offspring. The characteristics that an individual, or phenotype, acquires during its existence are therefore not part of the transmissible traits. A classical example of an acquired characteristic are the blacksmith's adapted muscles. According to modern genetics, the information needed to develop such muscles cannot be passed along to the blacksmith offspring. If the children want to take up their father's trade, they will have to develop their own muscles from scratch. It is of course debatable whether such a state of affairs is a good or a bad thing. Big and strong hands would certainly be an asset for a future blacksmith, but what if junior decides to be a pianist? Also, too much dependence on ready-made knowledge might impair an individual's ability to learn (and adapt) by himself.

The idea that acquired traits can be inherited was defended by the French naturalist Jean Baptiste de Monet, Chevalier de Lamarck, who lived between 1744 and 1829. Lamarck contributed some influential works on plants and invertebrates, but he is best known for his views on evolution, referred to as Lamarckism. His theory is based on the altogether plausible idea that plants and animals evolve by adjusting to changes in their environment, and that such changes can be passed on to the next generation. Lamarck's ideas clash head-on with Darwin's widely accepted theory of evolution, according to which variations in traits occur randomly at the chromosome level and not in direct response to changes in the environment.

Many of Lamarck's conceptions, such as the spontaneous creation of life, have been proven thoroughly wrong. But he still had followers well into the twentieth century, notably the Russian agronomist Trofim Lysenko, who convinced Stalin to denounce genetics as contrary to the principles of dialectical materialism and to establish

Lamarckism as an official Soviet doctrine. Leading Soviet geneticists were dismissed, jailed, or exiled. The result was a serious setback in genetic research in the USSR, further discrediting Lamarck himself for having his name associated with such a scientific fiasco.

Lamarckism may not have been part of nature's evolutionary plan, but it has a role to play in the adaptation of artificial systems. If genetic algorithms for solving the TSP are to be competitive, then the inclusion of some kind of Lamarckian ingredient seems unavoidable. In such a scheme, selection and crossover take place only after each individual in the population has "done its best," that is, it has computed a local minimum using some local optimization technique such as 2-Opt. This amounts to allowing the favorable traits that were acquired as a result of "experience" (local optimization) to be transmitted to the next generation.

A Genetic Solution for the TSP

Evolution is not destiny, it is opportunity! Its path is not predictable, but it can be controlled.
(H. Mühlenbein, M. Georges-Schleuter, and O. Krämer)[12]

Mühlenbein et al. described their algorithm as one way of jumping from local minima to still better local minima. Here are the main steps.

1. *Initial Population.* 16 tours are selected at random and assigned to 16 different processors.
2. *Improving the Fitness.* Each processor computes a locally optimal solution t' beginning with its present tour t (t' is the tour of minimal length that can be obtained from t by repeated application of 2-Opt swaps). The new, better solutions t' replace the original tours t.
3. *Selection of Mating Partners.* The processors are interconnected in a gridlike fashion in such a way that each one of them has four neighbors. At reproduction time, each processor mates its tour (the receiver) with some other processor's tour (the donor). The latter is chosen among the receiver's four neighbors plus the shortest tour overall (the "fittest" string in the current popula-

153

tion). These five potential donors have probabilities of 30, 25, 20, 15, and 10 percent of being selected—the shorter the donor tour, the higher the probability.

4. *Crossover*. A substring is chosen at random from the donor (the length of the substring should be between 10 and one-half the number of cities). The single offspring string begins with the donor substring followed by the rest of the cities in the order they appear in the receiver, as illustrated below.

0 1 2 3 4 5 6 7 8 9 (donor)　　　7 1 0 9 3 6 5 8 2 4 (receiver)

3 4 5 6 7 1 0 9 8 2 (offspring)

5. *Stopping Criterion*. The 16 offspring resulting from the 16 matings form the new generation. If a certain (predetermined) number of generations have passed without improving the best overall solution *s* (the shortest tour), the algorithm stops and returns *s* as "the" solution. Otherwise, steps 2 to 5 are repeated.

It is perhaps not surprising that both the quality of the solution and the speed of evolution increased with the size of the population, which ranged from 2 to 24 in the different runs. Experiments by other researchers suggest that for a given amount of computation time, the quality of the solution can also be improved by using a more powerful local optimization technique. This factor appears to be more important than population size, to the point where a recent genetic algorithm produced high-quality results with a population size of only one.[13] In such a scheme, mating is no longer possible, and variation must be obtained by random mutations alone. Ironically, such an exclusive reliance on mutation was blamed for the failure of the early attempts to mesh computer science and evolution. "In the late 1950s and early 1960, [these attempts] fared poorly because they followed the emphasis in biological texts of the time and relied on mutation rather than mating to generate new gene combinations," wrote John Holland in a 1992 article.[14]

In the final remarks of their report, Mühlenbein's team ponders over the role of natural systems as an inspiration for artificial models. "In tuning the evolution algorithms," they write, "we found that often the best parameter choices are those most similar to the parameters we find in nature." As an example, they observe that their genetic algorithms work best with two parents, instead of three or more. "Evolution algorithms can be very easily developed," they conclude, "but their behavior is complex. Evolution is not destiny, it is opportunity! Its path is not predictable, but it can be controlled." The last two sentences echo a philosophy that permeates the soft computing approach: in the absence of an exact theory, we may not be able to predict the future but we can still control it.

NOTES

1. John H. Holland, *Adaptation in Natural and Artificial Systems*, MIT Press, Cambridge, MA, 1992.

2. Ibid.

3. Anatol Rapoport and Albert M. Chammah, *Prisoner's Dilemma*, Univ. of Michigan Press (1965), p. vii.

4. Axelrod, R., "The Evolution of Strategies in the Iterated Prisoner's Dilemma," in *Genetic Algorithms and Simulated Annealing*, Lawrence Davis, ed., Pitman, London, 1987, pp. 32–41.

5. Stephen Jay Gould, *The Mismeasure of Man*, Norton, New York, 1991.

6. S. Lin and B. Kernighan, "An Effective Heuristic Algorithm for the Traveling Salesman Problem," *Oper. Res.* 21, 498 (1973).

7. S. Lin, "Computer Solutions of the Traveling Salesman Problem," *Bell Syst. Tech. J.* 44, 2245 (1965).

8. R. M. Brady, "Optimization Strategies Gleaned from Biological Evolution," *Nature*, vol. 317, 31 Oct. 1985, pp. 804–6.

9. Johnson and McGeoch, "The TSP: A Case Study."

10. H. Mühlenbein, M. Georges-Schleuter, and O. Krämer, "Evolution Algorithms in Combinatorial Optimization," *Parallel Computing* 7 (1988), 65–68.

11. Paul Feyerabend, *Against Method*, NLB, London, 1975, p. 49.

12. H. Mühlenbein, M. Georges-Schleuter, and O. Krämer, "Evolution Algorithms."

13. Olivier Martin, Steve W. Otto, and Edward W. Felten, "Large-Step Markov Chains for the TSP Incorporating Local Search Heuristics," *Operations Research Letters* 11 (1992), 219–24.

14. John H. Holland, "Genetic Algorithms," *Scientific American*, July 1992, pp. 66–72.

THE RELEVANCE of a new theory or idea is seldom easy to estimate, and its long-term consequences always risky to predict. This is true in every domain, and mathematics or computer science are no exceptions. In presenting the principles of soft computing I have therefore focused on widely accepted concepts and techniques that have been around for some time, staying away from the latest fad or the claims ("this may save the world") that have yet to live up to their promises.

At times I felt overwhelmed by the myriad of articles, books, and talks given at conferences around the world on the subject: Was I missing something crucial? But this very abundance served to reassure me. Perhaps the reason there are so many different approaches, special techniques, partial solutions, new ideas, etc., is that the definite theory (if such a thing exists) has yet to be found.

When comparing soft and classical computing, the following (partial) table may be useful:

Classical Computing	Soft Computing
needs a program up front	may learn its own program (NNs)
based on two-valued logic	uses many-valued logic (FL)
deterministic	incorporates random elements (GAs, NNs)
handles exact data	can handle ambiguous data (FL)
sequential computation	parallel computation (NNs, GAs)
precise answers	approximate answers (FL)

A characteristic common to fuzzy logic, neural networks, and genetic algorithms is their dependence on massive and fast calculations. For all the importance of the underlying mathematical theories, theory alone would be of little use without high-speed computing to put it into practice. Also, the role of technological marvels other than computers (sensors, spectroscopes, etc.) in the implementation of the theories cannot be overstated.

The three nonclassical approaches to computation I have discussed here are by no means the only ones being employed or developed. Genetic algorithms may be seen as a special case of a larger, still

ill-defined field known as evolutionary computing. Two other possibilities are biochemical computing, which uses proteins as logical gates and to store information, and the exploitation of chaos—a very popular theory merely a decade ago—that is artificially generated.

I do not wish to have given the false impression that traditional mathematics is not up to the task! A new domain where (crisp, exact) mathematics is currently being successfully used in computer science is program construction, where there is a growing interest in formal, mathematically based methods in the design of algorithms and for the development and verification of software.

Presently (i.e., in 1997) there is a trend toward so-called hybrid systems, combining the advantages of two or more methods or techniques. This is good news. I have met too many researchers who were convinced that only one approach (theirs, of course) held the key to the mysteries of the universe. Scientists may be well-advised to once again imitate nature and take advantage of the opportunities afforded by diversity, cooperation, and combination if their goal is to solve the largest number of problems for the benefit of the greatest number of people.

FUZZY INFERENCES

FUZZY INFERENCES AS MAPPINGS

A typical fuzzy inference rule has the form

if x is A and y is B then z is C

where A, B, and C are fuzzy subsets of the universes X, Y, and Z, respectively, that is, they are functions

$$A: X \rightarrow [0,1]$$
$$B: Y \rightarrow [0,1]$$
$$C: Z \rightarrow [0,1],$$

from the universes to the set $[0,1]$ of real numbers between 0 and 1.

A fuzzy inference rule is interpreted mathematically as defining a mapping from fuzzy subsets to fuzzy subsets. The fuzzy subset C' of Z corresponding to the pair A', B' of fuzzy subsets of X and Y, respectively, is, by definition,

$$C'(z) = \bigvee_{x \in X, y \in Y} A'(x) \wedge B'(y) \wedge A(x) \wedge B(y) \wedge C(z) \quad (1)$$

where $\vee$ denotes maximum (or supremum, if X or Y is an infinite set) and $\wedge$ denotes minimum.

DIGRESSION: FUZZY DEDUCTIONS AND MODUS PONENS

In classical logic, modus ponens is the name of the deduction rule by which the truth of the statement Q follows from the truth of both the conditional statement "if P then Q" and the statement P. This is usually written as

if P then Q

P

Q.

A fuzzy inference rule has the form of a conditional statement, so the temptation is great to see C' as arising from the conclusion of a "fuzzy" deduction by writing

if x is A and y is B then z is C

x is A' and y is B'

----

z is C'.

In the particular case $A' = A$ and $B' = B$, the above fuzzy deduction would be formally identical to modus ponens provided $C' = C$. Now, if $A = A'$ and $B = B'$ in (1), then

$$C'(z) = \bigvee_{x \in X, y \in Y} A(x) \wedge B(y) \wedge C(z)$$

and therefore C' is not necessarily equal to C. This fact has been interpreted by some as meaning that modus ponens breaks down in fuzzy logic. (Actually, if for some $x \in X$ and $y \in Y$ we have $A(x) = 1$ and $B(y) = 1$, then $C' = C$. The reader is invited to verify this.)

THE FUZZY OUTPUT

In the general case, there are n fuzzy inference rules:

if x is A_1 and y is B_1 then z is C_1

if x is A_2 and y is B_2 then z is C_2

...

if x is A_n and y is B_n then z is C_n.

The mapping defined by this set of rules associates to the input pair (A', B') of fuzzy subsets the fuzzy subset of Z defined by:

$$C'(z) = \bigvee_{\substack{x \in X, y \in Y \\ 1 \le i \le n}} A'(x) \wedge B'(y) \wedge A_i(x) \wedge B_i(y) \wedge C_i(z). \quad (2)$$

In fuzzy control applications, a set of fuzzy inference rules may be interpreted as a function $z = f(x, y)$ that cannot be neatly described by a mathematical equation. Suppose that the (numerical) input values are $x = x_0$ and $y = y_0$. These numbers are used to define the (ordinary) subsets $A' = \{x_0\}$ and $B' = \{y_0\}$ as functions in the usual way: $A'(x_0) = 1$, and $A'(x) = 0$ for $x \neq x_0$; $B'(y_0) = 1$, and $B'(y) = 0$ for $y \neq y_0$.

The right-hand side of (2) can now be simplified by observing that $A'(x_0) \wedge B'(y_0) = 1 \wedge 1 = 1$; and $A'(x) \wedge B'(y) = 0$ for all $(x, y) \neq (x_0, y_0)$, so that (2) reduces to

$$C'(z) = \bigvee_{i=1}^{n} A_i(x_0) \wedge B_i(y_0) \wedge C_i(z). \tag{3}$$

For example, if $n = 2$, (3) becomes

$$C'(z) = (A_1(x_0) \wedge B_1(y_0) \wedge C_1(z)) \vee (A_2(x_0) \wedge B_2(y_0) \wedge C_2(z)),$$

or

$$C'(z) = \max\{\min\{A_1(x_0), B_1(y_0), C_1(z)\},$$

$$\min\{A_2(x_0), B_2(y_0), C_2(z)\}\}.$$

DEFUZZIFICATION

The procedure that yields a single numerical value $z = z_0$ from the fuzzy output C' is known as defuzzification. The center of gravity method is one of the most popular. If—as it is often the case—the universe Z is finite, say $Z = \{z_1, z_2, \ldots, z_m\}$, then the center of gravity z_0 can be computed with the formula

$$z_0 = (z_1 C'(z_1) + z_2 C'(z_2) + \cdots + z_m C'(z_m)) /$$

$$(C'(z_1) + \cdots + C'(z_m)). \tag{4}$$

Together, equations (3) and (4) define the output $z = z_0$ from the input values $x = x_0$ and $y = y_0$. They constitute one of a number of sensible definitions of the mathematical function $z = f(x, y)$ described by a given set of fuzzy inference rules. Many variants of either the fuzzy output or the defuzzification method have been used in particular applications. For instance, defuzzification can also be achieved by choosing the number z_0 with the largest membership grade in C' (or their arithmetic mean, if there is more than one).

161

THE FUNCTIONS OF NATURAL NUMBERS CANNOT
BE ENUMERATED

*We show that there are more functions of natural numbers
than can be written down on an infinite list.*

LET N be the set of positive natural numbers: $1, 2, 3, \ldots$. Functions
from N to $\{0, 1\}$ may be represented by infinite strings of 0s and 1s in
a natural way. For example, the function

$$f(n) = 1, \text{ if } n \text{ is odd}; f(n) = 0, \text{ if } n \text{ is even},$$

becomes the string

$$1 \quad 0 \quad 1 \quad 0 \quad 1 \quad 0 \quad 1 \quad 0 \quad \ldots$$

of alternating 1s and 0s. In general, the function h is represented by
the string whose n-th entry is $h(n)$, that is,

$$h(1) \quad h(2) \quad h(3) \quad \ldots \quad h(n) \quad \ldots$$

We now prove that every infinite list of functions from N to $\{0, 1\}$
is incomplete. Suppose that L is such a list of functions. The first
entry on L is a certain function f_1, the second entry is a function f_2,
and so forth, that is, for each positive natural number n there is an
n-th entry on the list that we denote f_n. It is convenient to imagine the
functions written one below the other: first f_1 (represented by its
binary string), then f_2, and so on. We have thus an infinite matrix of
0s and 1s, such as, say

$$
\begin{array}{llllllllllll}
(f_1) & 0 & 0 & 0 & 1 & 0 & 0 & 1 & 1 & 0 & 0 & \ldots \\
(f_2) & 0 & 1 & 1 & 0 & 1 & 0 & 0 & 0 & 1 & 1 & 0 & \ldots \\
(f_3) & 1 & 1 & 1 & 0 & 1 & 1 & 0 & 0 & 0 & 1 & 0 & 0 & \ldots \\
\ldots \\
(f_n) & f_n(1) & f_n(2) & \ldots & f_n(n) & \ldots \\
\ldots
\end{array}
$$

The diagonal of this matrix is the binary string

$$f_1(1) \quad f_2(2) \quad f_3(3) \quad \dots \quad f_n(n) \quad \dots \qquad (1)$$

Now let g be the function defined, for each n in N, by

$$g(n) = 0, \text{ if } f_n(n) = 1;$$

$$g(n) = 1, \text{ if } f_n(n) = 0.$$

In other words, the string corresponding to g is obtained from the diagonal string (1) by changing 1s into 0s and 0s into 1s. For instance, assuming that the first three functions on the list are as illustrated above, the diagonal string begins 0 1 1 ..., so g begins 1 0 0 ...

This function g is not on the list L. For given any f_m on L, by the definition of g, we have $g(m) \neq f_m(m)$. Since g and f_m take different values at one natural number, namely m, they cannot be equal. The function g is therefore missing, so the given list is incomplete. Notice that it would do no good to try to fix the original list by including g on it. The argument given above applies to *any* list, so the new list would also be incomplete—some function other than g would be missing.

The functions from N to $\{0, 1\}$ form a proper subset of all the functions from N to N. Since the functions in the smaller set cannot all appear on a single list, *a fortiori*, no complete list of those in the bigger one can exist either.

THE HALTING PROBLEM IS UNSOLVABLE

*We show how to derive a logical contradiction from the
assumption that the halting problem can be solved by some
Turing machine.*

I T IS in principle possible to automatically encode the program of
any Turing machine as a single natural number. The details are not
important; it is enough to know that it can be done (actually in many
different ways). By selecting one specific encoding, we can assign to
each Turing machine a natural number—its code—from which the
machine's program can be recovered by an appropriate (automatic)
decoding. If a given natural number m happens to be the code of
some Turing machine, we designate this machine by $T(m)$. In other
words, $T(m)$ is the Turing machine (if there is one) whose code
number is m.

Suppose now that some Turing machine, H, say, solves the halting
problem in the following sense: H accepts as input a pair (m, n) of
natural numbers and it returns as output 1 if m is the code of a
Turing machine and this machine—$T(m)$—would eventually halt
after being started with the number n on its input tape. In any other
circumstances, H's output is 0. Once again: H writes a 1 at the end
of its computation if $T(m)$ stops on input n, and it writes a 0 otherwise—that is, if either m is not the code of a Turing machine, or m *is*
the code of a Turing machine, but this machine will never stop
computing on input n.

It is very easy to write the program of another Turing machine—let
us call it E—which stops immediately if its input is the number 1,
and enters an infinite loop if it started reading the number 0. By
connecting H and E "in series" (i.e., so that H's output becomes E's
input) we obtain a third Turing machine, C, which behaves as
follows: for each natural number n,

if $T(n)$—that is, the Turing machine with code n—does not stop on
input n, then C stops on input n;   (1)

if $T(n)$ does stop on input n, then—on input n—C goes into an
infinite loop and never halts.   (2)

Here we go again: on input n, C first uses H to determine whether $T(n)$ would halt or not if started on this same input n. Then C acts on this information to do precisely the opposite of what $T(n)$ would do: if the latter would eventually stop, C sets itself on a course to run forever; if, on the contrary, C "learns" that $T(n)$ would never halt, then C terminates its computation.

It should be clear that if H exists, so does C. Below we show that the (so far hypothetical) existence of C leads to a logical contradiction. Therefore, there is no such C, and so H cannot exist either.

For suppose that C is built as indicated. The program of C, once encoded, becomes *some* natural number, c, say—that is, $C = T(c)$. Now, let us start C on input c and consider what might happen. The behavior of C being specified by clauses (1) and (2) above, we can rephrase them with n (the generic input) replaced by the present input c. These clauses now read:

if $T(c)$ does not stop on input c, then C stops on input c, and

if $T(c)$ does stop on input c, then—on input c—C goes into an infinite loop and never halts.

But C and $T(c)$ are one and the same machine. Therefore, if C existed, it would have to both eventually stop and run forever *at the same time* on one of its inputs—a logical impossibility.

LEARNING WITH THE BACK-PROPAGATION ALGORITHM

THE back-propagation algorithm is designed to train feedforward networks composed of two or more layers of neurons, and connected so that the outputs from one layer become the inputs to the next one. In addition, the activation functions of the neurons must be continuous (to allow for the use of differential calculus). The algorithm derives its name from the fact that the weight adjustments dictated by the learning rules propagate "backwards," from the output layer towards the input layer.

To explain the principles of the algorithm we shall employ a modest network consisting of only two layers (fig. A.1). When the three neurons in the first (or hidden) layer receive inputs y_1 and y_2, they respond with intermediate, or hidden, outputs z_1, z_2, and z_3. These are then passed on to the two neurons in the second (output) layer, which transform the z_j into the final outputs o_1 and o_2 according to the usual formulas

$$o_i = f(s_i), i = 1, 2 \tag{1}$$

where f is the neuron's activation function (assumed to be the same for all neurons); s_i is the weighted sum

$$s_i = v_{i1} z_1 + v_{i2} z_2 + v_{i3} z_3 \tag{2}$$

and v_{ik} is the weight, or strength, of the connection joining the k-th input to the i-th neuron. The z_j are themselves computed in a similar way, by applying f to the weighted sum of the inputs y_1 and y_2

$$z_j = f(u_{j1} y_1 + u_{j2} y_2), j = 1, 2, 3. \tag{3}$$

After a given input pattern $y = [y_1, y_2]$ has been processed, the network responds with an output vector $o = [o_1, o_2]$. The response error E is then calculated by comparing o with the desired response, which is another vector $d = [d_1, d_2]$. More precisely, E is defined by

$$E = (d_1 - o_1)^2 + (d_2 - o_2)^2 \tag{4}$$

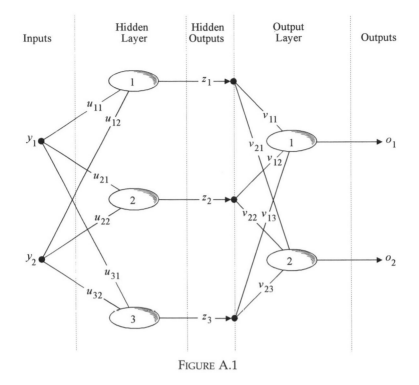

FIGURE A.1

that is, the sum of the squares of the local errors $d_k - o_k$ at each output neuron (since squares cannot be negative, adding the squares $(d_k - o_k)^2$ prevents negative local errors from off-setting positive ones).

From equations (1) to (4) follows that, for a given input y, the error E is a function of the weights only—twelve in this case. In other words, E assigns to each 12-dimensional weight vector w the number $E(w)$ specified in (4). In the simplest case, when E is a function of only two variables, w_1 and w_2, the error can be visualized as a surface in 3-dimensional space hanging above the 2-dimensional weight plane. Starting at any given point on this surface, there is one direction that corresponds to the steepest climb, or, equivalently, to the fastest rate of increase in error. Mathematically, this is the direction defined by the so-called gradient of error, a 2-dimensional vector ∇E whose components can be calculated using differential calculus (they are the partial derivatives $\partial E / \partial w_1$ and $\partial E / \partial w_2$). The error decreases most rapidly in the direction opposite that of ∇E, which is that of the vector $-\nabla E$. This is the direction of steepest descent. When the dimension of the weight space is greater than two, such a neat geometrical interpretation is impossible. But the opposite gradient vector $-\nabla E$ still "points" in the direction of fastest error reduction, and so, by analogy, it is customary to always speak of "steepest descent."

If we denote by w some initial (perhaps randomly chosen) weight vector, then $E(w)$ is the error for these particular weights. Now, since continuous neurons can respond with any number between 0 and 1, it is very unlikely that the network outputs o_1, o_2 (for given y and w) will exactly match the desired ones d_1 and d_2; in other words, $E(w)$ will almost certainly be different from zero. The algorithm must then calculate a new weight vector w', ideally so that the error is reduced as much as possible. But E is generally a complicated function of many variables, with many unknown (and possible unknowable) features. This makes the search for the optimal weights a formidable task, the path toward the minimum error being most likely long and plagued with deceptive pseudo-solutions—the feared local minima already discussed in chapter 6. Given the scant information available about E, the algorithm's best move in the circumstances would be to update the weight vector in the direction of steepest descent...and hope for the best.

The choice of the new weight vector w' is therefore dictated by the imperative to reduce the error as rapidly as possible. Thus, a weight increment Δw that moves the current weight w along the direction of steepest descent must be computed. Starting with the output layer, the algorithm calculates the components of Δw layer by layer. A kind of "error signal" traveling backwards, from output to input, enters into the calculation of the weight increments—hence the algorithm's name: error back-propagation. After the weights have been updated (i.e., the old weight vector w replaced by the new one w', where $w' = w + \Delta w$), the next input pattern is fed to the network and the weight adjustment process begins all over again. Once the training cycle has been completed—that is, after all patterns in the training set have been tested—the errors arising from the individual patterns are added. If this overall error is smaller than a preset threshold, the training is complete; otherwise, a new training cycle begins.

In a nutshell: back-propagation may be described as an efficient technique for calculating the gradient error in one sweep through the network, working with only one input pattern at a time. For all the talk about training, learning, synapses, signal propagation, and so forth, it is really differential calculus and vector algebra working behind the scenes that get the job done.

After receiving his Ph.D. in mathematics from the University of Montreal in 1971, ARTURO SANGALLI has taught and done research at various colleges and universities in Canada and abroad. His fields of interest include mathematical logic and the use of novel methods for the analysis and resolution of conflicts, from labor relations to international disputes. He is also active in the popularization of mathematics and its applications, and has been for many years a contributor to the British weekly *New Scientist*. In 1996, he won the Author of the Year Award from the French Canadian Association for the Advancement of Science (ACFAS). He is presently in the Department of Mathematics at Champlain Regional College, in Lennoxville, Quebec.

* Index *